Flights of Victory
Vuelos de Victoria

Ernesto Cardenal

ERNESTO CARDENAL

FLIGHTS OF VICTORY
VUELOS DE VICTORIA

edited and translated by
Marc Zimmerman

with Ellen Banberger and the collaboration of
Mirta Urróz, Eileen Sutz, Renny Golden, Patricia Carlos,
Carlos Bauer, Edward Baker, and María Teresa Ayala

CURBSTONE PRESS

*Thin
p.*

9560
23·04·91.
c

Reissued by Curbstone Press, August 1988
Originally published by Orbis Books, Maryknoll, NY

Library of Congress no. 84-5278
ISBN 0-915306-74-3

distributed in the United States by
THE TALMAN COMPANY
150 Fifth Avenue
New York, NY 10011

CURBSTONE PRESS
321 Jackson Street, Willimantic, CT 06226

Contents

IV VUELOS DE MEMORIA Y VISIÓN
FLIGHTS OF MEMORY AND VISION

Preface

Most of the poems in this collection appeared first in Nicaraguan newspapers and then either in *Nicaráuac: Revista Cultural* of Nicaragua's Ministry of Culture or in *Poesía Libre*, the publication of the ministry's literature section. Two poems, "Aterrizaje sin epitafio" and "A Ernesto Castillo mi sobrino," appeared in Cuba's *Casa de las Américas*. Many of the poems were also published in the beautiful Spanish edition, *Tocar el cielo* (Wuppertal, Germany: Peter Hammer Verlag GmbH; Salamanca, Spain: Lóguez Ediciones, 1981). Finally, some others were sent to me in manuscript by Ernesto Cardenal and may not have appeared to date.

To the best of my knowledge, the only poems presented here which have appeared in authorized English language collections of Cardenal's works are "La llegada" and "Luces," both of which were published in Cardenal's *Zero Hour and Other Documentary Poems* (New York: New Directions, 1980).

Of all the works collected in this volume, only "Amanecer," "La llegada," "Las campesinas del Cuá," "En el lago," and "Vuelo sobre la patria sin escala" were completed before the Sandinista victory of 19 July 1979. These exceptions are included here because they are among the writings Cardenal has published thus far about the final years of the insurrection against Somocismo and are otherwise appropriate in theme and technique to this collection. Above all these poems appear here because Cardenal felt that this book would be an incomplete reflection of his recent work without them. Not in spite of but because of the "repeat performances" of "Luces" and "La llegada" (in translations different from those published by New Directions), this volume may claim to provide the best and most direct followup to previously published Cardenal collections by presenting a complete picture of his poetic development during the years of Nicaragua's insurrection and reconstruction.

The genesis of this book is worthy of mention, if only to indicate how collaborative work may be promoted and how the enthusiastic participation of young, relatively inexperienced students may yield valuable results for themselves and for those who are the receptors of the final product. The volume was first conceived as a joint student/community project of LUCA (Latinos, University, Community, and Art), a program of the Rafael Cintrón Ortíz Cultural Center for Latino students, which I coordinate at the University of Illinois at Chicago. It was, in fact, an offshoot of a planned sequel to a book I edited with Bridget Aldaraca, Edward Baker, and Ileana Rodríguez,

Nicaragua en revolución: Los poetas hablan/Nicaragua in Revolution: The Poets Speak (Minneapolis: MEP, 1980). I first made rough drafts of some translations and then distributed most of them among my collaborators, who reworked them. Patricia Carlos, Eileen Sutz, and Mirta Urróz, students of mine, were the first to be involved in the process. Carlos Bauer and especially Ellen Banberger did exceptional work on several of the poems; Ed Baker allowed us to publish his translations of "Las campesinas del Cuá" and "Luces" and suggested some modifications in Banberger's drafts. Renny Golden helped revise an early version of the introduction, helped secure publishing rights from Cardenal, and gave important editorial advice on the volume as a whole. Ernesto Cardenal sent me copies and revisions of new poems and indicated what he hoped would be included. María Teresa Ayala, a student, helped with several translations of poems Cardenal sent us after our initial text was set for publication. Ultimately, of course, I made the final revisions and corrections and gave the book the shape it now has; I am responsible for any defects that may be found.

I wish also to acknowledge the help of Margaret Randall, who gave advice to Renny Golden and me about the project; to Edna Padilla, cultural center secretary, and Sylvia Solís, a Latin American Studies student, for their help in preparing the manuscript; and to Professor Leda Schiavo for acquainting me with and allowing me access to *Tocar el cielo*.

These recent poems by one of the great revolutionary poets of Central and Latin America are dedicated to the loftiest aspirations of a people's struggle and to the fallen who helped make the revolution and national reconstruction possible. Their translation, as well as my introduction, is also so dedicated with the hope that Cardenal's view of the new Nicaragua, seen in the context of his overall vision of cosmic hope and redemption, may permeate the minds and hearts of those whose primary language is English. The publication of these poems, at a time when many are seeking to undermine Nicaragua and its revolution, should be taken as an act of commitment, a call to further solidarity with the cause of a beleaguered people.

INTRODUCTION

Ernesto Cardenal after the Revolution*

Cardenal and the Flights of Poetry

Commentators on Nicaragua's history have observed that the Nicaraguan people are particularly inclined to travel and flight. The phrase *de viaje* is a national byword, and from ancient times there have been those who have had to take flight: those pre-Columbians who left their footprints in Acahualinca as they fled the erupting volcano; those who fled the conquistadores or fled the first U.S. invaders led by William Walker, the slaver who declared himself president of Nicaragua in the late 1850s; those who, like poet Rubén Darío, chose to leave for international cultural centers or used their poetry for flight; those who fled the U.S. military occupation from 1912 to 1925 and again in 1927 (until it was the invaders who Sandino's army forced to flee, though they left a National Guard that would incite future flight); those who fled one of the earthquakes that destroyed Managua; those who fled into exile to escape one or another bloody Somoza; those peasants and revolutionaries caged in helicopters and dropped on garbage dumps or onto mountain crags or into the Momotombo volcano itself; those who went off into the mountains to bury the heart of the enemy; those who raised material aid and launched solidarity drives by flying from place to place to tell the story of the Sandinista struggle; those who flew to Costa Rica to enter the Southern Front; and finally all those who flew into Sandino Airport that first year of victory to take part in the most arduous flight of all: the reconstruction.

Like so many other Nicaraguans, Ernesto Cardenal has always been fascinated with flying and soaring, with birds, with wings, with airplanes and all planes: with skies, aerial views, the moon, the stars, the Milky Way, and all the ecstasies and terrors of flight. Of course all his poems have been flights into the Nicaraguan past or into the heart of Central American life. So in his

---

*A somewhat different version of this essay was read at a conference on politics and poetry at Illinois Wesleyan University on 2 April 1982.

ix

"Canto nacional" ("Nicaraguan Canto") Cardenal weaves Sandinista visions with the flights and sounds of Nicaragua's native birds. So he writes of aerial views in his "Viaje a Nueva York" ("Trip to New York"). So he writes in "Oráculo sobre Managua" ("Oracle over Managua") of Leonel Rugama's Apollo poems and of planes bringing food and clothing the Somozas confiscate; in "Las campesinas del Cuá" he speaks of peasants dropped from helicopters; in "La llegada" he writes of landing and dreaming of socialism while confronting the customs agents of Somoza's Nicaragua.

Then too all of Cardenal's many poems, long and short, are imbued with religious and ethereal flights. The poems contain views from the promised land. There are visions of time and space, of unity between the most mundane details of concrete living and the most spiritual dimensions of cosmic being, and of an achieved identity between the gospel's kingdom of heaven and socialism's kingdom of this world.

In Cardenal's spiraling flights of poetic invention, the work of Nicaragua's vanguardists with their turn from Darío's *modernismo* to the national reality, the work of Ezra Pound with his method of collage (as well as his sense, however reactionary, of epic, world-historical relations), and the work of Neruda with his all-encompassing Latin American vision come together with Thomas Merton, Teilhard de Chardin, and other masters of spiritual voyage in a new synthesis which Cardenal called *exteriorismo* and which in its most advanced articulation may be considered the point where all sources find their place in the construction of a Sandinista "aeronautics" of poetry.

In the early 1970s, prior to his overt commitment to the Sandinista cause, Cardenal wrote:

> *Exteriorismo* is a poetry created with images of the exterior world, the world we see and sense, and that is, in general, the specific world of poetry. *Exteriorismo* is objective poetry: narrative and anecdote, made with elements of real life and with concrete things, with proper names and precise details and exact data, statistics, facts, and quotations. . . .
> In contrast, interiorist poetry is a subjectivist poetry made only with abstract or symbolic words: rose, skin, ash, lips, absence, bitterness, dream, touch, foam, desire, shade, time, blood, stone, tears, night. . . .
> . . . I think that the only poetry which can express Latin American reality and reach the people and be revolutionary is exteriorist. . . .
> Poetry can serve a function: to construct a country and create a new humanity, change society, make the future Nicaragua as part of the future great country that is Latin America.[1]

Exteriorismo became the poetry par excellence of a nationalist resistance to Somoza in the name of Sandino. It was a poetry influenced by the great vanguardists of Nicaragua (José Coronel Urtecho, Joaquín Pasos, Pablo Antonio Cuadra, Manolo Cuadra) and also by the great revolutionary poets of other Central American countries (Otto René Castillo of Guatemala, Roque Dalton of El Salvador); a poetry filled with culturally loaded objects, with national names and places, with local references and linguistic idiosyncracies—all there to underline and counteract the incursions and distortions of destructive and lying master-powers. The very prosiness of exteriorist poetry, its ever-open, narrative, metonymic mode of discourse, its very refusal of the overtly poetic, metaphoric, pristine, and symmetrical made it the perfect vehicle for a realistic evocation of a horrendous reality. Indeed, *exteriorismo* was the ultimate fulfillment of Huidobro's call, taken up by the vanguardists and given new, radical meaning by Cardenal and the many young Nicaraguan poets who were to follow him:

> Por qué cantais la rosa oh poetas!
> Hacedla florecer en el poema!
>
> Oh, poets, why sing of the rose!
> Make it flower in your poems![2]

This was to be the major task of *exteriorismo:* to convert the vanguardist project of concrete, objectivist poetry into one by which poetry would transcend its own productive mode and help transform the very world it sought to render—to bring the rose of poetry to the Sandinista struggle, transforming poetic expression by taking on the weight of the Sandinista historical experience and fertilizing the seeds of revolutionary aspirations so that they might flower in the field of action.

In the hands of Cardenal, Fernando Gordillo, the young Leonel Rugama, and the scores of now known and still unknown Nicaraguan poets who participated in the creation of this increasingly honed politico-cultural instrument, *exteriorismo* was, for all its surface realism, for all its materiality and concreteness, the expression of a core idealism with respect to life, possibility, and hope. The harsh sounds of torture sessions and shootouts, the glare of National Guard searchlights and raw-bulbed Sandinista cell meetings all came together and were explicitly juxtaposed to a standard of truth and humanity. The alienation of verses, like the alienation of objects, people, and families, was the counterpart of a diametrically opposed vision—a vision that was Rousseauesque in one dimension (the values of the seignorial countryside over the capital-penetrated cities) but was, in another dimension, deeply religious and communal. In the massive transmutation of values implicit in Cardenal's violent juxtapositions and montages, the seemingly uncultivated peasants struggling to oust the imposed powers were the true keepers of a spirit that would shine like the light of Sandino over the sinister tropical nights of the Somozas. This light would rise from the inferno of dictatorships, repression, and defeat to illuminate a transcendent, revolutionary force that was born in the Age of Reptiles and would fulfill its teleological itinerary in the creation of a new and radiant humanity.

Cardenal: The Trajectory of His Flight before the Victory

Cardenal was born on 20 January 1925 in Granada, Nicaragua. He earned his high school diploma at the Colegio Centroamérica in his hometown and then went on to study literature, first in Managua, and then, from 1942 to 1946, at the National Autonomous University of Mexico (UNAM), where he received his degree by presenting a series of essays on Nicaraguan poetry. From 1947 to 1949 he took graduate courses at Columbia University in New York and then spent over a year traveling in France, Italy, Spain, and Switzerland. He returned to Managua in 1950 and there came into contact with opponents of the regime of Anastasio Somoza García, who had become the virtual dictator of Nicaragua in 1936. The group Cardenal joined was made up of young people from "good," conservative families, much like Cardenal's own. Their meetings led to the abortive April Rebellion of 1954, headed by Adolfo Baez Bone and Pablo Leal. The conspiracy was betrayed early on, and the two leaders, as well as several other close friends of Cardenal, were killed. Cardenal left the country. In May 1957 he entered a Trappist monastery located in Gethsemani, Kentucky.

This decision to study theology and eventually become a priest surprised virtually all who knew Cardenal as a promising young poet with very strong political convictions. He had begun publishing his poems in the 1940s, culminating his early phase with a series of famous epigrams modeled on Catullus and very openly attacking Somoza García. But Cardenal's subsequent concern with seeing worldly events in the frame of a transcendent religious perspective hardly emerges in this early work. It seems quite probable that various dimensions of his background, and most especially his experience in the April Rebellion, led to his turn toward religion. In any event, the death of Baez Bone is a theme of one of the most solemn and profound of his epigrams, and the rebellion itself, linked to the overall history of Nicaragua and the figure of Sandino, is a constituent theme of Cardenal's great poem "Hora cero" ("Zero Hour"). Indeed, the themes and images of "Hora cero" would permeate his subsequent writing; combined with a religious dimension that was soon to emerge, these themes and images would be essential to the poetic armature of Cardenal's later committed, Sandinista poems and would carry over into his postvictory poetry.

At Gethsemani, Cardenal served as a novice under the famous poet-priest Thomas Merton. The two men came to know and translate each other's poetry, and the influence of Merton on Cardenal was considerable. However, Cardenal's health was too fragile to endure the demands of Trappist discipline. He left the monastery in 1959, studied theology in Cuernavaca, Mexico, and then in 1961 traveled to Colombia, where he continued his religious studies. He also continued writing poetry throughout these years, publishing *Gethsemani, Ky.* in 1960 and *Salmos* (Psalms) in 1964. These works, especially the latter, established his reputation and marked the first full interaction of politics and religion in his poetic universe.

The period of Cardenal's stay in Colombia corresponded with the growing influence of liberation theology, as it would later be called, among the younger priests in Latin America. Camilo Torres, one of the most influential figures of this new mood and movement, was very active in Colombia. Cardenal admired Torres's decision to give up his ministry and join Colombia's guerrilla movement, even though the choice'of arms was something the young poet could not imagine for himself. However, even prior to joining the priesthood, Cardenal was influenced greatly not by the church hierarchy, which still took a stance toward political life that favored the ruling classes, but by those who saw the political situation in much of Latin America as an affront to their religious values and the possibilities of human salvation.

On 15 August 1965, at the age of forty, Cardenal was ordained a priest in Managua. But some months earlier, on 13 February of the same year, he and two friends, William Agudelo and Carlos Alberto, had arrived at the archipelago of Solentiname and had founded a Christian commune based on certain conceptions that had their roots in the teachings of Merton. A group of thirty-eight tiny islands in Lake Nicaragua, Solentiname then had a total population of under one thousand peasants and fisherfolk. It was during the Solentiname years (1965–77) that Cardenal merged the artistic, political, and religious dimensions of his life's work. He and his friends established a church and commune which they named "Our Lady of Solentiname." Each Sunday the peasants, fisherfolk, and their families came to participate in the Eucharist and to dialogue and comment on the Gospels. Gradually, various collective workshops formed—most notably ones devoted to art and poetry—in which the people of Solentiname participated and grew. Gradually, too, the political orientation of the gospel studies deepened.

In its theory and practice, the Solentiname community was developing a mode of life that drew on idealized conceptions of the early Christians and on the utopian conceptions of pre-Marxist socialists. These dimensions emerge in the art works and poems produced in Solentiname during the first years of the commune; an even richer and more complex image emerges in *El evangelio de Solentiname* (Salamanca: Ediciones Sígueme, 1975), which was translated and published as *The Gospel in Solentiname* (Maryknoll, N.Y.: Orbis Books, 1978). Cardenal's own development may be traced in the works he produced in the early years: *El estrecho dudoso* (1966) and *Homenaje a los indios de América* (1969). This latter text derived from Cardenal's studies of pre-Columbian Amerindian cultures. He came to believe that the classic Mayan cities were peaceful, classless societies whose values coincided with and actually enriched the Christian ways he was seeking to propagate in Solentiname. However, what seems lacking in Cardenal's view was a historicist perspective on how the classic Mayan cities fell and how the values Cardenal had come to admire might reemerge in modern society. Such a perspective would only emerge later.

The first phase of the Solentiname years was marked by a Mertonian adherence to the principle of nonviolent opposition to all forces preventing a realization of the kingdom of heaven on this earth. However, circumstances were to alter this situation. First, there was the general development of the Sandinista movement throughout Nicaragua in the late 1960s; second, there was the earthquake of 1972 and the attendant intensification of Somocista exploitation and oppression. As for Cardenal himself, his trip to Cuba in 1970 may be seen as a decisive moment that would result in a qualitative transformation of his mission in Solentiname and of his political and poetic stance.

Cardenal went to Cuba to serve as a judge in a poetry contest sponsored by Casa de las Américas. There he became aware of the possibility of building a society that met basic needs and rejected exploitation. Invited to stay a few weeks, he ended by staying three months, visiting all parts of the island, talking to everyone he could. As testimonial to his experience, he polished his copious notes and published them in the book *En Cuba* (In Cuba). In this text Cardenal looks critically at certain aspects of Cuban society, but he is struck by what he considers to be the fundamentally Christian orientation of this overtly anti-Christian revolution. As he puts it in a recent letter (to this editor and dated 19 Nov. 1984): "I never considered the Cuban Revolution to have lacked a Christian basis, but rather that this revolution was the Gospels put into practice, and what had to happen was for the Christians in Cuba to understand this revolution." According to Robert Pring-Mill, Cardenal after his Cuban trip believed that "the New People 'that is going to be born' would be a people made up of the New Men whom Che Guevara predicated, but the values of their 'communism' would coincide with those of the earliest Christians."[3]

This was the vision which gradually came to answer the questions Cardenal left unanswered in *Homenaje a los indios de América* and which informed Cardenal's work in Solentiname as the Somoza regime became increasingly rapacious in the years following the earthquake in Managua. Solentiname was a living counterculture to the world of Somoza, an anticipation of what Nicaragua could be after Somoza. But it was also to become one of the training grounds for active struggle against the dictatorship.

By the early 1970s Cardenal had already begun to diverge from the Mertonian ideal of strict nonviolence because, as he was to say, "In Nicaragua, as in other parts of Latin America, nonviolent struggle is not possible." In this period he dedicated his "Canto nacional" to the Sandinista National Liberation Front, but he still spoke of nonviolent struggle; and it was not until the mid-1970s that he was actively supporting the revolutionary projects of the Sandinistas in his poetry, his public speeches throughout the world, and his continuing work in the Solentiname community.

Of the transformation in Cardenal's work during this period, José M. Valverde writes:

Poetry ceases to be his primary experience and central interest, so that poetry may give itself to the service of life itself, of a life consecrated to something beyond itself: to solidarity with the oppressed and to the love of God, each time in greater unity. Stylistically this makes Ernesto Cardenal's poetry more tied to its themes, to things, to others, forgetting intimacy. . . . Even without losing any of his literary knowledge, Cardenal has simply come to distance himself from classifications and analysis by his commitment to apostolic and political action.[4]

A crucial poetic document of these years is Cardenal's "Oráculo sobre Managua" which brings together the postearthquake expropriations by Somoza with the life story of the poet-militant Leonel Rugama, a seminary student who turned poet and then Marxist guerrilla fighter. Rugama wrote poems contrasting U.S. Apollo flights to the moon with the poverty of Managua barrios, only to die in 1970 during a seemingly futile shootout with the National Guard in one such barrio. But in postearthquake Managua Cardenal was eager to see the reincarnation of Rugama's evolution and ultimate revolutionary spirit in the hearts of Nicaragua's young people. Something of the sort occurred in Solentiname as young disciples moved from a religious, nonviolent stance to one which inclined toward militant action.

By October 1977 the Solentiname commune had turned Sandinista. And on 12 October the young people joined in an armed attack on National Guard military installations in the town of San Carlos on the border with Costa Rica. The guard was defeated, and the San Carlos port fell into the hands of the insurgents. But shortly thereafter, the guard, using its airplanes, launched a counterattack that placed the civilian population in danger. The Sandinistas decided to retreat to avoid a massacre. In this sequence of events some of the Solentiname young people died, others were sent to prison, and others sought refuge in Costa Rica. Cardenal's community was liquidated; all the communal buildings were destroyed except for the church, which was converted into a guard barracks.

Some days earlier Cardenal had left Solentiname to go on a tour for the Sandinistas. Word reached him of the destruction of his community and of the fact that his special immunity under Somoza was at an end. Declared an outlaw, Cardenal published an open letter about the assault and the destruction of Solentiname, and he sent off a second communiqué proudly declaring himself as an active member of the Sandinista movement. In an important text of 1976, he writes:

I became politicized by the contemplative life. Meditation is what brought me to political radicalization. I came to the revolution by way of the Gospels. It was not by reading Marx but Christ. It can be said that the Gospels made me a Marxist. . . .

. . . It can be said that all the young people of Nicaragua are today leftist extremists, all the young people who think they are interested in social and political problems. Even fifteen-year-old girls educated in colleges run by nuns, devout Christians, are today supporters of communism, without seeing any conflict between the Marxist revolution and Christianity.[5]

Written in the wake of Solentiname's destruction, Cardenal's "Open Letter to the People of Nicaragua" indicates that collective meditation on the social relevance of the Scriptures had played a leading role in the radicalization of his commune, ultimately inspiring its members to join in the armed struggle "for one reason alone: out of their love for the kingdom of God. Out of their ardent desire for a just society, a true and concrete kingdom of God here on this earth."[6] After the destruction of Solentiname, Cardenal went on one speaking tour after another in Latin America, Europe, and the United States, raising money for the Sandinista movement and winning new recruits for solidarity work. He also took part in deliberations over the new reconstruction government that formed in Costa Rica and readied itself to take power after the fall of Somoza. In his letter he summarized his position at this time: "I have given no thought to the reconstruction of our little community of Solentiname. I think of the far more important task, the task for us all: the reconstruction of the whole country." On 18 July 1979 Cardenal and other newly appointed government officials flew in from San José, Costa Rica, to Nicaragua to begin carrying out the task about which the poet-priest of Solentiname had written and dreamed.

Nicaragua, Cardenal, and His Poetry after the Victory

As an anonymous reporter for the Managua-based publication *Amanecer* points out, *before* and *after* are the essential adverbs in the current flight of Nicaraguan reconstruction. The reporter writes, "Political, social, and economic activity, as well as many dimensions of daily life, have changed. The revolution has rebaptized streets and buildings, has changed offices and officials, has transformed neighborhoods and whole cities."[7] The before and after categorizations apply as well to Nicaraguan culture and to the poet-priest who heads the Ministry of Culture and spearheads the cultural revolution; the contrasting categorizations are in fact one of the dominant themes of his "after" poems.

"It was an audacity of this revolutionary government," says Cardenal, "to create a Ministry of Culture while having on its hands a nation in ruins and bankruptcy and with priority needs such as health, housing, food, and education. From the beginning culture was also considered to be a priority."[8]

And so the house that *before* was the private reserve of Somoza's wife came *after* the revolution to be the center for the work of popularizing the national culture. And Ernesto Cardenal, before the shepherd of Solentiname, became the shepherd of Nicaragua's cultural revolution.

From the beginning he saw the aim of his work as the "democratization of culture":

> To bring culture to the people who before were marginalized from it. We want a culture that is not the culture of an elite, of a group that is considered "cultivated," but rather of an entire people.[9]

Thus, soon after assuming office, Cardenal directed the construction of cultural houses and workshops, developed a national magazine, and carried out innumerable steps for the dissemination and development of the people's culture. After little more than a year of work he could say:

> Before our people shocked the world with their struggle, and now the world will be startled by our cultural development. . . .
> . . . The cultural houses have multiplied all over. Our folklore, which before was in decadence, has resurged extraordinarily in every area of the nation. Popular theater, mainly by workers and peasants, blooms in every province, and the same with song and music. . . . Our people have expropriated their culture, which before was marginalized and is now their own, as they are owners of their land and their historical destiny.[10]

And all of this took place while the government attempted to solve all the basic problems Cardenal pointed to—while it carried out massive literacy and health campaigns, while it had to deal with the gravest economic and political problems. And, furthermore, the cultural revolution advanced while the United States put increasing pressure on the Sandinista government, while it blocked financial assistance, while it sent in CIA operatives and right-wing mercenaries, while it encouraged counterrevolutionary businessmen who drained capital from the economy, while it infiltrated the news media and fomented disorder among Nicaragua's black and Indian populations, while it supplied and financed deadly incursions from across the Honduran border, while it launched an overall campaign to discredit and destabilize the Nicaraguan Revolution.

What happened to poetry in the midst of these developments? Before the revolution Cardenal had led the way for the poets of Nicaragua by forging a poetry that not only expressed but in fact contributed to the formation of a broad, anti-imperialist counterculture which, centered on the image of Sandino, ultimately united otherwise disparate sectors in a broad coalition that toppled the dictatorship. After the victory a key question was how long the broad-based unity could last: how long could the euphoria of revolution keep together sectors which had ultimately different historical projects and goals. A related question, of course, was what would happen to the counterculture itself and to the foremost expressive mode of that culture. Indeed, since Darío, poetry had been the center of Nicaraguan cultural creation; given a religious dimension by Cardenal and then becoming the basis of a popular musical movement through the work of the Mejía Godoy brothers and others, poetry had served as a key nexus between the radical, revolutionary sectors and the people. What would happen to poetry, to exteriorist poetry, and to the poetry of *exteriorismo*'s prime exponent when such poetry was no longer the counter but the dominant mode, when its prime inspiration (Somoza's negative now turned to Sandino's positive) was no longer in power?

As for Cardenal himself, what would happen when he no longer led the counterculture but was given the task of creating a new cultural world? Motivated by the liberation theology which he had helped to forge and by the exteriorist poetic mode which he had been instrumental in developing, Cardenal had found the solution for his search for the kingdom of heaven on earth in *Sandinismo*. Heaven was the light of Sandino in its triumph over the night of Somoza; the materiality of objects, animals, people, and language itself could serve to realize a spiritual quest that found its extrapoetic correlative in the revolution. What would happen to Cardenal's work when Somoza was no longer present? Would Cardenal's poetry have the same dynamic tension and power? What would be the thematic and imagistic source of this poetry? Would Cardenal continue to write a critical, political poetry? Would he continue to be one of Latin America's most important poetic voices? How would his work be affected by the effort to build a new nation, to develop a broad, national culture, and to fend off the dominant classes? Would his poems reflect his having to do battle against old allies (including fellow poets and churchmen, friends, and colleagues) who were not happy with the new order? What would be the effect on his own poetic production of his new role as government official and leader in the development of a culture traditionally dominated by poetry and song?

A few months after the Sandinista victory, Cardenal commissioned Mayra Jiménez, who had been the poetry specialist at Solentiname, to launch a series of popular poetry workshops throughout the country. Shortly after Cardenal could boast that many workshops had been established, and workshop poems began to appear in the Sandinista newspaper, *Barricada*, as well as in the ministry's own journal, *Nicaráuac*. Indeed, by the end of 1982 the workshops had entered into the areas designated for activity after the literacy campaign and into the heart of every new structure created by the revolution. In this context Cardenal could boast:

> The production of new poetry is startling. There are poetry workshops in the poorest neighborhoods, in factories, in the army and even in the police precinct offices. I think that Nicaragua is the only country in the world where poetry produced by the police is published.[11]

And yet like everything else that has emerged since the Sandinista victory, Nicaragua's poetic production is a matter for constant commentary and debate. Daily the controversy escalates over the results of these poetry workshops. Some claim that the uncodified and ever-changing principles of revolutionary *exteriorismo* have now taken on an academic, institutionalized air and have become a "prolet-cult" style that is a standard for the writing of poetry. Many young Nicaraguan poets seem intent on imitating every superficial aspect of Cardenal's poetic style and orientation, and a rigid posture of "revolutionary virtue and commitment" is said to dominate and stultify national poetic production.

Truly there has been some imitation, posing, and sheer banality in this new poetry. And yet some valuable work has already emerged from the efforts of these young poets. And their staunch defender, Ernesto Cardenal, is quick to point out that the publication and even criticism of these first poems by young men and women should lead to a deeper and more extensive development of national cultural life. Meanwhile, in the midst of his own many tasks—his coordination of the arts, his political duties, his public speaking engagements, his budget reviews and sessions of program planning and evaluation, as well as his many flights throughout the national territory and abroad—Cardenal has continued to write his own poetry.

Given all he has had to do—the struggle to develop his own ministry, to contribute to national development, and also to fend off the attacks that have come his way from within his own church—the very fact of this poetry's existence is remarkable. It is all the more remarkable if we consider the way Cardenal had been accustomed to write his poetry. Early in the reconstruction period, Robert Pring-Mill noted:

> Whether Cardenal will be able to write much poetry while Minister of Culture seems doubtful, particularly since his accustomed method of composition involves long periods of meditation: drafting, redrafting, cutting up, and re-assembling numerous versions, on the way toward the final process of montage (often working on several poems in parallel, with the composition of the longer ones sometimes lasting over several years). He told me in San José, just after his appointment to his ministerial post, that he could see no way to get back to this kind of work till he could withdraw from public politics, adding that he could not write poetry in any other way.[12]

Furthermore, the construction of new poems is not simply a matter of time, energy, and method. There was the whole question of how to transform his poetic instrumentalities in relation to the new postvictory situation. There was the whole question of what was functional and what was not in relation to a changing social reality. What would happen when an instrumentality designed for criticism and attack would now be placed at the service of what Cardenal had every intention to serve and support? Would Cardenal the poet become subject to Cardenal the minister? Would his own work come to be influenced by the workshop simplifications and imitations of a rich and fresh poetic mode he previously had helped to forge?

Clearly Cardenal's poems after the victory provide a measure for Pring-Mill's prediction and the basis for answering the questions we have raised.

Cardenal's Flights of Victory

As noted in the preface, although all but five of the poems in this volume were completed after the victory, most of the poems refer to previctory matters. In addition to their poetic resonance and documentary significance, the previctory poems included have the virtue of allowing readers to make comparisons of Cardenal's poetry *before* and *after* 19 July 1979 on the basis of what is presented in this volume. However, the poems are presented here not according to their date of completion or publication; given Cardenal's method of working on several poems at the same time, this would not have been very revealing in any event. Rather, the poems are organized according to narrative, historical, and thematic continuity. This approach should enable those concerned with Cardenal's work to follow in a fairly logical and coherent manner the elaboration of the poet's dominant preoccupations and methods; furthermore this approach serves to delineate Cardenal's view of Nicaragua's recent historical development.

The poems readily group themselves into four sections according to their major unifying theme, *flight*. The first group, "Flights of Insurrection," provides a picture of the struggle against Somoza as it developed and deepened in the 1970s. While dealing with the last months of the insurrection, "Ofensiva final" stands as an introductory evocation because its references to poet-combatant Leonel Rugama along with the images of moonflight link this entire group of poems to Cardenal's previctory concerns: religion, the kingdom of heaven, the cosmos, revolution, and the poet as mediator between humanity and the universe. The earliest poem, "Amanecer," from 1972, introduces the Sandinista preoccupation with light and dawn as symbolic motifs of the revolution as the poet evokes the passing of the evil demons of the night and the possibility of a new day. "La llegada," a poem of 1974, reveals Cardenal's already nearly complete identification with the Sandinista struggle at a time when, still protected by his international standing, he could enter Nicaragua and go on with his work. The poem is one in which ritual business, such as plane flights and customs checks, begins to emerge as a central motif.

Based on an actual occurrence, "Las campesinas del Cuá" is not only a crucial document but also a fine poem summarizing Somocista oppression of peasants in the northern mountains as more and more communities became part of the Sandinista struggle and as dreams of revolutionary victory began to dominate the popular imagination. The poem inspired a song by Carlos Mejía Godoy which became very popular in Nicaragua and throughout the world, to the point that it actually served as a rallying cry for solidarity and direct involvement in the insurrectional process; the poem has taken on an added significance now, given the Sandinistas' problems and bad press with respect to some members of Nicaragua's rural, indigenous populations.

"En el lago" brilliantly elaborates the cosmic dimension of Cardenal's vision of the October 1977 raid on San Carlos, Nicaragua, in which members of the Solentiname community participated and after which the community was destroyed. Next, in "Vuelo sobre la patria sin escala" we read of Cardenal's flight over the same lake and the entire nation as he views the damage of Somocista firebombings in the wake of the September 1978 uprising. He ponders the devastation of the town of Estelí, and, passing over Solentiname, he dwells on the destruction of his community by the Somocistas during the previous year, as he heads for a conference where he will ask for the kind of international support the revolution requires. "Muchachos de 'La Prensa' " and "Barricada" return us to the concrete details of the events of May–July 1979 that finally brought down the Somoza regime. But even in these very specific poems so rooted in the events they describe, the particular enmeshes with the world-historical (for example Cardenal's references to ancient Greece and Rome) and universal.

Part II, "Flights of Victory and Celebration," begins with four poems that present a collage of flight, landing, and arrival. We then go with the poet through the streets of Managua to a series of mass rallies which Cardenal portrays with a mixture of realism and mystic vision, culminating in his sense of a new, limitless, yet to be determined freedom which he can only characterize by elaborating on the ubiquitous Sandinista image of a "new dawn." The first of the flight poems, "Luces," is a fine work in the line of Cardenal's great epics. It is apparently the first poem he completed after the victory of 19 July and has a special historical import in describing the secret flight from Costa Rica which brought in leaders of the new Sandinista government to the newly liberated country.

But "Luces" is only one of several remarkable poems in this section. Another is "Aterrizaje con epitafio" with its evocation of the fallen and its striking closing lines:

The wheels now only a few meters off the ground.
And a voice over the microphone should say: Ladies and Gentlemen
the ground we are about to touch is very sacred.
. . . The wheels have just landed, passengers,
on a great tomb of martyrs.

Through their mystical evocations, the celebration poems also hold their fascination by transcending mere testimony to the early demonstrations. All faces become one face, and one hand comes to stand for all hands from the beginning of human evolution to the present moment of rejoicing and consecration. As part of the process, we see the women from Cuá now telling their story directly to the people. The two final poems give us visions of boundless possibilities and hopes. A single phrase of an unnamed revolutionary commander sets off a series of thoughts (and, as Cardenal adroitly adds, this phrase is just one of many); a morning journey through the countryside evokes the vision of a new life for the poor and oppressed.

Part III, "Flights of Reconstruction," begins with an overview of the many tasks to be accomplished during the first months of the reconstruction and then moves with Cardenal himself through a series of encounters and experiences that tell us about his activities and preoccupations as Minister of Culture—and of course about the revolutionary process in its varied domestic and international dimensions. In effect, after the poem "Ocupados" we are presented with a very busy day. We start and end in Managua at night. But the time between the two night poems constitutes a kind of synoptic, twenty-four-plus-hour day in the life of a revolutionary process. We follow Cardenal through the city, into the Segovia Mountains, out to the Pacific Coast, and to several points of the national territory; next we're off to Quito, Düsseldorf, and the island of Grenada; then it's back to the bordertown of Somoto, to the outskirts of Managua, and finally to Cardenal's own bedroom at home. Throughout this long day's journey we encounter the theme of humankind and all the species caught up in a biological, historical, and cosmic process that has its culmination in revolution and reconstruction.

In the first of these poems we see Cardenal on his way at night to a meeting. Here, in "Reflexiones de un ministro," we have the conflict between poetry and politics and between private and public that Pring-Mill anticipated would impede Cardenal's artistic production. Cardenal, the poet with pure poetic inclinations, wants to study a cat that appears in his path, wants to write a poem about the cat but cannot because Cardenal, the religious/revolutionary minister, must go to his meeting. The poet is repressed, we are told, but we are told this in a poem that takes the supposed conflict between poetry and politics as its subject matter and transcends the apparent impasse. Of course the poet's circumstances and commitments determine the kind and quantity of poetry he will write, but we should note that this little poem is one of the most playful and carefully crafted (in the Marianne Moore sense) of Cardenal's recent work. It is also the poem which announces pressing matters that are central to Cardenal's poetic orientation during the reconstruction: that the personal and a concern for all the species of the world be integrated in a poetry that is necessarily focused on broad sociohistorical and political issues. In both content and form "Reflexiones" confirms Cardenal's relation to the Anglo-American poetic tradition even as it shows the poet taken up with the demands of national development and the poetic forms that would correspond to it.

If, in the instance cited, duties of state prevent the poet-minister from dwelling on a fellow creature of the animal kingdom, other instances require the greatest preoccupation with the species of our world. Thus, we next see

Cardenal at an emergency cabinet meeting where for love of one's neighbor all leading state functionaries must focus on a particular kind of mosquito. Relations with one's neighbor and with nature itself emerge in all of these poems, as Cardenal begins his voyage around the national territory and then out into the wider world beyond. In this early phase of reconstruction, the poet sees the peasant women and all the people of Cuá living in a state of jubilation; the entire animal kingdom and indeed all of nature are also benefiting from the reconstruction. Moving from the Atlantic to the Pacific area, Cardenal sees the procreation of a turtle and the celibacy of a dedicated priest such as himself as both having a role in the ecological life cycle. Then, at a conference in Ecuador, random thoughts by the priest lead to a vision which links the struggles of Bolivia and El Salvador in a larger process extending from the iguana. A mass in faroff Germany evokes the rallies in Managua as well as the spirit of Solentiname and Nicaragua's reconstruction. A rally held in Grenada several years before the events of 1983 again joins nature and humankind, and Grenada and Nicaragua (like the turtle and the priest), together in a struggle against foreign forces of destruction. The theme of imperialism persists as we follow the poet to the dangerous border area between Honduras and Nicaragua where his parable about parrots evokes the tradition of Darío (*"Tantos millones, hablarémos inglés?"*) and reminds us how the question of Nicaragua and Central America's cultural and human future is still tied to U.S. as opposed to evolutionary or divine designs. The revolution has its serious problems, but on the outskirts of Managua Cardenal has recollections and then a comic "mystic vision" that confirm his faith in the process. Finally at home in bed after his journey into the new world of reconstruction, Cardenal thinks of those who died in the struggle and feels they have not died in vain, that in spite of the problems the revolution is doing fine.

Thoughts of the past and visions of the present and future, as well as the preoccupation with the animal, human, and overall physical world in the total "nature of things," persist in the fourth and final section. Starting with a poem that evokes the worldview of the contemplative priest in the early days of Solentiname, "Flights of Memory and Vision" projects its fundamental themes in terms of key issues, moments, and figures in the distant and recent national history seen from the perspective of the national reconstruction in progress. Thus Juan's questions to Cardenal are projected in relation to the young man's present participation in voluntary work and the militias; Cardenal portrays the young Sandino's encounter with the iguanalike *garrobos* as the Sandino Museum is under construction; his reminiscence of Rigoberto López Pérez, the national hero who "executed" Anastasio Somoza García in 1956, is colored by the goals of the reconstruction to do away with a society which created drunks and beggars; his memory of Mother Ana, a lovely girl who became a reactionary nun, seems provoked by the growing split among church people over the revolution.

The same orientation persists as we move to a group of poems about those who have died as Sandinista militants. Cardenal's memory of Donald Guevara and Elvis Chavarría (as well as Felipe Peña), members of the Solentiname poetry group who died in the San Carlos assault or afterwards, points to the reconstruction efforts carried out in the name of the dead—but also includes a barb against any dogmatic priest (even the archbishop of Managua) who would deny that such young fallen combatants live on; a second poem, to Elvis alone, takes up the poet's thoughts about the turtle in the Pacific and is imbued with Cardenal's sense of mission (and the mission of Elvis)—to give life, though neither can have a child; his memory of Ernesto Castillo, a young poet-combatant killed in the insurrection, is informed by many of the concrete goals and achievements of the revolution, not the least among them the new military élan and the poetry workshops where many young people follow the path of both Ernestos, uncle and nephew, in writing militant poetry. A final poem of particular recollection, "Viaje muy jodido," refers to those dying in the struggle against the counterrevolutionaries in the border areas. But the poem, at the same time one of Cardenal's most irreverent and reverent, also ties our images of the fallen to the core figure of Rugama while extending beyond the realm of the poets and the realm of Solentiname to all Nicaraguans and all those struggling in the Caribbean-Central American zone.

The two general poems to unnamed and unknown soldiers which follow bespeak Cardenal's sense of purpose even in the midst of death and universal desintegration; the second of these poems, "En la tumba del guerrillero," projects us out again toward universal space, where even the eventual destruction of the planet will not mean that those who died in the revolution died in vain but rather that all truly human endeavor will endure as particles of light in the eternal evolution of the vast and irreducible cosmos. The poem in question is a major work; its philosophical and imagistic richness takes us back to many of the other important poems in this volume which suddenly achieve a new complexity and significance.

But what is also remarkable in this section as well as the one before it is the strong personal note which registers in the shorter, "lesser" poems. Such poems, starting with "Reflexiones de un ministro," take us back to some of Cardenal's works written in his earliest years of productivity, when influences from the Nicaraguan and Latin American poetic tradition were mediated by the work of writers like William Carlos Williams and Marianne Moore. The new poems show that the master of revolutionary epic and intergalactic poetic flight can still relate intimate, subjective details in comic as well as serious ways, even as he is caught up in national, world-historical, and cosmic-religious themes. Far removed as at least a few of these shorter poems may seem from Cardenal's standard mode of writing, they mark in fact an enrichment of *exteriorismo*, in that the subjective and even the humorous can find their space not in opposition to but within the framework of a poetic approach aimed at objectification and expansion.

The penultimate poem returns us to the happier dimension of Cardenal's historic vision—his sense of joy over the revolutionary victory, his conviction of its crucial, impermeable nature in the cosmic scheme of things. Then a final poem, "Visión de la ventanilla azul," depicts Cardenal flying off once more, looking out through his window over the homeland as he did in his flight of 1978; seeing the scenes of battle, of fallen heroes; seeing that now all is blue as he flies off—with thoughts of religion, Nicaragua, and revolution—on his way to his next destination, wherever it may be.

Theme, Technique, and Achievement
in Cardenal's Recent Poetry

Cardenal's recent poems mark a transition for his writing, as well as for his life and the life of the Nicaraguan people. Yet—perhaps surprisingly, perhaps not—we find little surface change in his basic themes or poetic techniques. The concern for concretion, for the things of the streets, for the chiclet sellers, shoeshine boys, and all the exploited, suffering ones of Acahualinca and Barrio San Judas is still present and so are the fusion of history and imagination, the merging of crude realism and soaring romanticism, the mystical equation of socialism and Christian communalism, the unifying vision of a new and loving humanity.

As for subject matter, Benjamin Forcano provides a useful summary:

Cardenal sings of the guerrilla fighter who gave his life for love and sings of the Sandinista final offensive, dangerous, foreseen, and unforeseeable but realized without error like a journey to the moon; the great barricade in which all the people put their streetstones, the luminous heroism in the nocturnal nights of Nicaraguan towns and villages, the ecstasy of the liberated homeland, the beauty of nature without Somoza, the joy of Waslala now without the wild beasts in camouflage uniforms, the ecological liberation of the rivers, lakes, trees, and animals. . . . Above all, Cardenal sings of the longing for communion with the universe, of a classless future society in which we will all love each other, of the need to change the heart and above all the system, [and of the necessity to create a world] where there is no longer exploitation, . . . where the earth is no longer in the hands of a few, where there will be resurrection because if not, how will those who died before the revolution be liberated?[13]

What most enables us to measure this poetry *after* with respect to Cardenal's poetry *before* is the fact that several of the poems, in whole or in part, clearly and consciously relate to or cite prior poems and motifs. Thus "Ofensiva final" harkens back to Cardenal's tribute to Rugama in "Oráculo sobre Managua"; "Vuelo sobre la patria sin escala" makes overt reference to the flight passages in "Viaje a Nueva York"; "Otra llegada" makes an explicit contrast with "La llegada"; "Llegaron las del Cuá" and "Waslala" both derive from "Las campesinas del Cuá"; "Ecología" and "Fundación de la Asociación Latinoamericana para los Derechos Humanos" draw on Cardenal's "Canto nacional"; "En la tumba del guerrillero" and indeed all the poems to the fallen harken back to a poem of the 1950s, "Epitafio para Adolfo Baez Bone," as well as to the Baez Bone section of "Hora cero." Perhaps least directly and most richly, "Luces" reviews the motifs of several poems while centering on the light of Sandino, the core image of "Hora cero."

Indeed, the thematic and imagistic consistency stemming from Cardenal's "macrovision" and permeating all of his major poetry persists throughout the poems written after the victory. Perhaps even more than from the Bible, from the teachings of Merton, or from the writings of kindred poets, Cardenal's vision would seem to stem from the work of Teilhard de Chardin, for whom matter is eternal light whose source is a love that wends its way through time and space, through the vicissitudes of biological evolution and historical revolution. In "Hora cero" the image was simple and conventional enough:

> What's that light way off there? Is it a star?
> It's Sandino's light shining in the black mountain.
> . . . .
> It's midnight in the Segovia Mountains.
> And that light is Sandino! A light with a song. . . .[14]

But the image follows Cardenal through his extended religious-poetic-political transformation and culminates in the complex play of light as we find it in several of the poems written after the victory. Again, the most significant transformation is the enmeshing of light with the theme of evolution—of a biological, historical, and cosmic process having at its center a Christian teleological perspective which Cardenal traces, almost obsessively, from its beginnings with the iguana, through the night of Somoza, and to the dawn of Che's new person, who finds fulfillment, union, and love in the revolution. This theme, often implicit in Cardenal, has one of its clearest enunciations in "Canto nacional":

> I said iguanas lay their eggs . . . It is the process. They
> (or else the frogs) in the silence of the carboniferous age
> made the first sound
> sang the first love song here on earth
> sang the first love song here beneath the moon
> it is the process.
> The process started with the stars.
> New relations of production: that too
> is part of the process. Oppression. After oppression, liberation.

> The Revolution started in the stars, millions
>   of light-years away. The egg of life
>   is one. From
> the first bubble of gas, to the iguana's egg, to the New Man.
> Sandino was proud he had been born "from the womb of the
>   oppressed"
>   (that of an Indian girl from Niquinohomo).
> From the womb of the oppressed the Revolution will be born.
> It is the process.[15]

It is a short step from this vision to "Oráculo sobre Managua" where "Revolution is a function of evolution itself / because . . . / evolution has a frightening velocity. / From a stick came light,"[16] and where Cardenal predicts, "We enter into the Easter of the Revolution," where "we shall be reborn together as men and as women. / It becomes a chrysalis and the / chrysalis sprouts wings."[17] Working from that point, we can begin to fully comprehend and integrate all the references in the poems after the victory—references to light, to iguanas, to *garrobos,* to process, to ecology, and to what, perhaps disturbingly for many North American readers, Cardenal insists on calling "communism."

If we turn from theme and image to Cardenal's overall expressive mode, we may say once more that his recent poems mark no sharp technical break—this in spite of the strong personal note that is struck in several of his reconstruction poems. True, there are no larger forms here, a fact that Pring-Mill's prediction of limited poetic production helps explain. But in generally more limited and condensed ways, we have here all the techniques which Pring-Mill identifies as basic to what he designates as Cardenal's "documentary" poems.

For Pring-Mill, Cardenal "set[s] out to 'document' reality (and so redeem it)" by "selecting, shaping, and imposing interpretative patterns on the world" and by making liberal use of techniques that can be likened to what we find in filmmaking and editing.[18] Cardenal employs

> shifts of focus or of angle; cuts from close up or detail shots right through to extreme long; jump-cuts for the sake of concision and abruptness; the poetic equivalent of pans and zooms; deft insert shots (to give additional data); the use of flashbacks (and flash-forwards), or of bridging shots . . . ; foreshortening and forelengthening, applied both to space and to time . . . ; studied relational editing; match-cuts which link two disparate scenes by the repetition of an action or a shape (or a sound)—but most of all the dialectical process of "collisional" montage, which generates fresh meaning out of the meanings of adjacent shots. . . .
>
> All these devices, together with Poundian textual collage and the full

range of more traditional poetic or rhetorical effects, are used in the course of Cardenal's documentary "redemption of reality," which successively "corroborates," "debunks," or "mediates" things, people, and events . . . from the standpoint of his brave new revolutionary world.[19]

Furthermore, Cardenal's poems

all aim at surface clarity, being meant for a wide public. They are strictly "factual," but . . . Cardenal's reader . . . has to visualize sequences of disparate images, . . . noting their pairings and progressions, matching them both with each other and with what is left unsaid—and thereby sharing in the extraction of their fuller "meaning."[20]

Finally, Pring-Mill writes that

Cardenal's recording of the present or the past is aimed at helping to shape the future—involving the reader in the poetic process in order to provoke him into full political commitment, thus fostering the translation of the poet's more prophetic visions into sociopolitical fact.[21]

All of these observations seem perfectly germane to Cardenal's poetic production after as well as before the Sandinista victory. His recent poems, like his earlier ones, are testimony to his unchanging belief that literature and poetry should be at the service of humanity. Also, like his poems before the victory, Cardenal's recent writing appears prosaic, digressive, purposely jagged, and disequilibrated. There are seemingly unaccountable tense shifts and line and spacing dispositions; there are seemingly awkward integrations of materials, as if the poet had afterthoughts which he has simply not tried to intermesh with his primary structures. But the purpose of all this is to create a multiplicity of planes and perspectives, to jar the reader, to refuse easy aesthetic harmonies, to provoke commitment, not applause, to demand completion not in literature but in life.

If before the victory Cardenal sought a language and expressive modes suitable to a broad audience, this seems even truer in several of the poems, especially the shorter ones, he has written since becoming Minister of Culture. In this we may perceive Cardenal's sense of responsibility to the larger sectors of his own society that have been recently brought to a level of minimal literacy. But a decision to write "for the people" is to risk the parochial, the trite, and all the ordinariness which is part of daily life. Possibly this explains why Cardenal may seem to miss his effect sometimes through an oversimplification of issues; why even the shorter poems may seem too explicit, tending toward an overflow of images, a proliferation of examples, explanations, and repetitions, as if he is not quite sure of his readers' understanding or belief and feels he must go over matters again and again.

Oversimplification is perhaps the most serious problem since it may necessitate repressing certain complexities in order to achieve a striking effect or evoke the reaction which is most readily in keeping with Cardenal's sense of political and spiritual priorities. Cardenal is clearly more preoccupied with the people's discovery of its own voice and life in his poetry than with a need to give intellectual, cultural, and literary respectability to the revolution. But his poems after the victory do pose certain problems which may have less to do with his poetic language and style than with his ability to grasp the complex forces at work in his native country.

The standard, negative critique of such poetry would suggest that Cardenal's affirmation of the revolution may seem too positive, exaggerated, and uncritical; his celebration of the revolution may appear as too ecstatic—as if based on wish and dream rather than reality. His vision would seem to lack dialectic, lack a willingness to express negative dimensions and doubts about the revolutionary process. In his recent work, the inevitable argument goes, there would seem to be too complete a sense of positivity which fails to take hold because it does not fully incorporate, account for, and therefore ultimately neutralize the negativities or doubts which must come with every process, no matter how affirmative, with every attempt to equate the spiritual and material, the hoped for and actual. The absence of alienation and doubt threatens the image of integration and affirmation projected by the poetry.

In his earlier poetry, such as "Oráculo sobre Managua," Cardenal could maintain at least a sense of negative possibility—of eradicating those forces that impede society's evolution toward the kingdom of heaven on earth. But this sense that Cardenal generally could grasp as a dimension of the historical process (after all, he has told us, if all of history were a day, the period of capitalism would last only ten seconds) is precisely what would seem to be missing in the recent poems. All is all too joyous in Waslala, in spite of all the real difficulties of integrating the Miskito Indians into the revolutionary process. The real leap from insurrectional victory to the solution of all the problems of a backward, struggling, multiethnic, fragmented country is too easy. And while Cardenal's postvictory opus includes several works that will ever be crucial to an overall study of his poetic career, there are other poems that are slight indeed, too readily showing the effects of their occasional, situational composition, as if they were written much as the poems say they are written: in airports, on airplanes, at conferences, in between meetings.

However, the shortcoming of these poems is not just that some of them are less developed than many of Cardenal's earlier works. Rather, they seem to suffer from a certain static quality; they partake of a pictorial as opposed to a narrative or dramatic orientation for which no amount of cinematic quick-cutting can compensate. Too often there is more talk about and praise of a process than actual depiction of the process in action. And it seems that Cardenal has been less able to grasp the decisive contours of the reconstruction than he was of the revolution. Indeed at times he seems to soar *over* the reconstruction without fully and firmly touching the ground.

Of the more outstanding, dynamic, and multidimensional poems, only "En la tumba del guerrillero" contains a sense of pessimism and negation which the poem simultaneously seeks to overcome—but even here, the reasons for pessimism seem writ into the nature of matter and the cosmos. Ultimately, we are led to ask if Cardenal has not fallen into the kind of strident, one dimensional yea-saying of which critics of his national poetry workshops have complained; we are led to ask if *exteriorismo* can only criticize the Somoza world and not the Sandinista problematic.

There is, however, another way of understanding the recent poems, just as Pring-Mill suggests we must understand at least parts of the poems written before the victory: that is, in counterpoint to their silences. Should we not see these poems as affirmative answers to the negative conditions which have threatened Nicaraguan reconstruction from its earliest days? Most of these poems were written, after all, as Somocistas and counterrevolutionaries massed on the Honduran border and carried out deadly incursions into Nicaraguan territory. Economic, political, and military interference from the United States—ranging from naval blockades to hit-and-run destruction of bridges, from covert infiltration and destabilization to increasingly overt and massive intervention—forms an ominous constellation of forces against which Cardenal's affirmative poems may be said to pose a profound, undaunted faith in the revolution and in the people's capacity for resistance and victory. More personally, the poems represent an arsenal in the struggle between those in the church who support the revolution and those who follow the church hierarchy; they are Cardenal's respectful, worshipful gesture before the admonishments of his pope.

Finally, in defense of these poems we should ask if it is not a legitimate task of a committed revolutionary writer to forge new myths rich in hope and possibility. Is it not correct for revolutionary poets to use their power of imagistic and rhythmic construction to pose a world more rich and beautiful than reality itself? At a time when so many opponents of Nicaragua's revolution are so quick to criticize every aspect of the Sandinista enterprise, is it not right for committed poets to practice their old, essential magic of not merely expressing but helping to create the reality they envisage—the reality they sense as potential in the reality that is?

This is a romantic conception, without doubt. But it is perhaps realistic and necessary. Indeed, *Flights of Victory* presents us with creative and vivid testimonies not to the concrete processes of "insurrection and reconstruction" but to the hopes animated by those who participated with the greatest enthusiasm and the most radical élan. Cardenal may not have had the time or sustained creative drive to elaborate a complex epic on the scale of "Hora cero," "Canto nacional," or "Oráculo sobre Managua"; he may not have had the leisure or peace of mind to fashion poems of creative observation à la

Marianne Moore; however, arranged according to their internal logic, the poems in this collection constitute a fragmentary but ultimately rich and coherent epic of Nicaraguan hopes and aspirations in the period of insurrection and reconstruction. As such this body of poetry is not only important in itself but also as a prototypical expression of a large sector of Nicaraguan and Central American writers, who in turn speak for still larger social aggregates. In fact, what today may distinguish Cardenal most from the other Nicaraguan and Central American practitioners of *exteriorismo* is his extreme capacity to respond to the particularities and necessities of history, politics, and everyday life within the context of an overriding macropoetic conception that combines religious and cosmic dimensions with a strongly particular and personal note, and articulates hopes and perspectives shared by great numbers of people with the most diverse interests and views.

As for the task of forging a poetry more able to portray the problems of revolution while still remaining revolutionary, of forging a genuinely critical revolutionary poetry: that endeavor still would seem to await many transformations of Nicaragua's material and ideological life, as well as of its poetic apparatuses. We can be sure that in these transformations the affirmative, visionary poetry written by Cardenal in the immediate period of insurrection, victory, and reconstruction, the poetry of ecstatic spiritual flight and vision, will remain an essential dimension and contributant.

MARC ZIMMERMAN

Notes

1. Ernesto Cardenal, ed., *Poesía nueva de Nicaragua: Selección y prólogo de Ernesto Cardenal* (Buenos Aires: Lohlé, 1974), 9–11.
2. For an examination of the impact of this passage on Nicaraguan poetry, see my "Pablo Antonio Cuadra y Leonel Rugama: Dos poetas, dos poéticas y dos políticas," *Taller* (León, Nicaragua), no. 16 (1981).
3. Robert Pring-Mill, "The Redemption of Reality through Documentary Poetry," introduction to *Zero Hour and Other Documentary Poems* by Ernesto Cardenal (New York: New Directions, 1980), xii–xiii.
4. José M. Valverde, prologue to *Antología* by Ernesto Cardenal (Barcelona: Ediciones Laia, 1978).
5. Ernesto Cardenal, *La santidad de la revolución* (Salamanca: Ediciones Sígueme, 1976), 20, 28.
6. See "Conversation between Brothers," *Movement*, no. 35 (1978), 3–4. Cardenal's "Open Letter" is followed by a letter, "Guns Don't Work," from Daniel Berrigan to Cardenal.
7. "Con Ernesto Cardenal," in *Amanecer: Reflexión Cristiana en la Nueva Nicaragua* (Managua, 1981), 15.
8. Ibid.

9. Ibid.

10. Ibid., 3, 16.

11. Ibid., 16.

12. Pring-Mill, "Redemption of Reality," xvi.

13. Benjamin Forcano, prologue to *Tocar el cielo* by Ernesto Cardenal (Wuppertal, Germany: Peter Hammer Verlag GmbH; Salamanca: Lóguez Ediciones, 1981), 11.

14. Cardenal, *Zero Hour*, 7.

15. Ibid., 20.

16. Ibid., 49.

17. Ibid., 51.

18. Pring-Mill, "Redemption of Reality," ix.

19. Ibid., xx-xxi.

20. Ibid., x.

21. Ibid.

I

VUELOS DE INSURRECCIÓN
FLIGHTS OF INSURRECTION

Ofensiva final

Fue como un viaje a la luna
con la complejidad y precisión de todos los detalles
contando con todo lo previsto
                    y también lo imprevisto.
Un viaje a la luna en el que el menor error podía ser fatal.
"Aquí Taller"—"Aló Asunción"—"Aló Milpa".
"Taller" era León, "Asunción" Masaya, "Milpa" Estelí.
Y la voz calmada de la chavala Dora María desde "Taller"
diciendo que los refuerzos del enemigo los estaban rodeando
peligrosamente,
la voz cantarina y calmada,
          "Aquí Taller ¿Me están escuchando?"
Y la voz de Rubén en Estelí. La voz de Joaquín en "Oficina".
"Oficina" era Managua.
"Oficina" no tendría municiones en dos días más ("Cambio").
Instrucciones precisas, en clave, dónde sería el aterrizaje . . .
Y Dora María: "No tenemos bien guardada la retaguardia. Cambio".
Voces serenas, calmas, entrecruzándose en la frecuencia sandinista.
Y hubo un tiempo en que el equilibrio de las dos fuerzas se mantenía
y mantenía, y estaba siendo muy peligroso.
Fue como un viaje a la luna. Y sin ningún error.
Muchísimos trabajando coordinados en el gran proyecto.
La luna era la tierra. El pedazo nuestro de la tierra.
Y llegamos.
Ya empieza, Rugama, a ser de los pobres; la tierra ésta
(con su luna).

Final Offensive

It was like a voyage to the moon
with complexity and precision in all details
accounting for all that was foreseen
                              and also what was not.
A voyage to the moon in which the slightest mistake could be fatal.
"Workshop here"—"Come in, Assumption"—"Come in, Cornfield."
"Workshop" was León, "Assumption" Masaya, "Cornfield" Estelí.
And the calm voice of Dora María, the girl from "Workshop,"
saying that enemy reinforcements were circling in
dangerously,
the voice sing-song and calm,
            "Workshop here. Do you read me?"
And the voice of Rubén in Estelí. The voice of Joaquín in "Office."
"Office" was Managua.
"Office" would be out of ammunition in two more days ("Over").
Precise instructions, in code, where the landing would be made . . .
And Dora María: "We don't have the rear guard well-guarded. Over."
Serene, calm voices intermixing on the Sandinista frequency.
And there was a time when the two forces stayed
even, and the danger was growing and growing.
It was like a voyage to the moon. And with no mistakes.
So very many coordinating their work in the great project.
The moon was the earth. Our piece of the earth.
And we got there.
Now it begins, Rugama, to belong to the poor; this earth
(with its moon).

Amanecer

Ya están cantando los gallos.
        Ya ha cantado tu gallo comadre Natalia
        ya ha cantado el tuyo compadre Justo.
Levántense de sus tapescos, de sus petates.
Me parece que oigo los congos despiertos en la otra costa.
Podemos ya soplar un tizón—Botar la bacinilla.
        Traigan un candil para vernos las caras.
Latió un perro en un rancho
        y respondió el de otro rancho.
Será hora de encender el fogón comadre Juana.
La oscurana es más oscura pero porque viene el día.
        Levántate Chico, levántate Pancho.
Hay un potro que montar,
        hay que canaletear un bote.
Los sueños nos tenían separados, en tijeras
tapescos y petates (cada uno en su sueño)
        pero el despertar nos reúne.
La noche ya se aleja seguida de sus ceguas y cadejos.
Vamos a ver el agua muy azul: ahorita no la vemos. —Y
esta tierra con sus frutales, que tampoco vemos.
Levántate Pancho Nicaragua, cogé el machete
hay mucha yerba mala que cortar
        cogé el machete y la guitarra.
Hubo una lechuza a medianoche y un tecolote a la una.
        Luna no tuvo la noche ni lucero ninguno.
Bramaban tigres en esta isla y contestaban los de la costa.
Ya se ha ido el pocoyo que dice: Jodido, Jodido.
Después el zanate clarinero cantará en la palmera,
        cantará: Compañero
                Compañera.
Delante de la luz va la sombra volando como un vampiro.
        Levántate vos, y vos, y vos.
(Ya están cantando los gallos.)
        ¡Buenos días les dé Dios!

4

Dawn

Now the roosters are singing.
      Natalia, your rooster's already sung, sister,
        Justo, yours has already sung, brother.
Get up off your cots, your bed mats.
I seem to hear the congos awake on the other coast.
We can already blow on the kindling—throw out the pisspot.
      Bring an oil lamp so we can see the faces.
A dog in a hut yelped
      and a dog from another hut answered.
Juana, it's time to light the stove, sister.
The dark is even darker because day is coming.
      Get up Chico, get up Pancho.
There's a horse to mount,
      we have to paddle a canoe.
Our dreams had us separated, in folding
cots and bed mats (each of us dreaming our own dream)
      but our awakening reunites us.
        The night already draws away followed by its witches and ghouls.
We will see the water very blue; right now we don't see it. —And
this land with its fruit trees, which we also don't see.
Wake up Pancho Nicaragua, grab your machete
there's a lot of weeds to cut
      grab your machete and your guitar.
There was an owl at midnight and a hoot owl at one.
      The night left without moon or any morning star.
Tigers roared on this island and those on the coast called back.
Now the night bird's gone, the one that says: Sc-rewed, Sc-rewed.
Later the skylark will sing in the palmtree,
      she'll sing: Compañero
        Compañera.
Ahead of the light goes the shade flying like a vampire.
      Wake up you, and you, and you.
(Now the roosters are singing.)
      Good morning, God be with you!

La llegada

Bajamos del avión y vamos nicaragüenses y extranjeros
revueltos hacia el gran edificio iluminado—primero
Migración y Aduana—y voy pensando al acercarnos
pasaporte en mano: el orgullo de llevar yo
el pasaporte de mi patria socialista, y la satisfacción
de llegar a la Nicaragua socialista—"Compañero". . .
me dirán—un compañero revolucionario bien recibido
por los compañeros revolucionarios de Migración y Aduana
—no que no haya ningún control, debe haberlo
para que no regresen jamás capitalismo y somocismo—
y la emoción de volver otra vez al país en revolución
con más cambios cada vez, más decretos de expropiaciones
que me cuenten, transformaciones cada vez más radicales
muchas sorpresas en lo poco que uno ha estado fuera
y veo gozo en los ojos de todos—los que quedaron
los otros ya se fueron—y ahora entramos a la luz
y piden el pasaporte a nacionales y extranjeros
pero era un sueño y estoy en Nicaragua somocista
y el pasaporte me lo quitan con la cortesía fría
con que me dirían en la Seguridad "pase usted"
y lo llevan adentro y ya no lo traen (seguramente
estarán telefoneando—seguramente a la Seguridad
a la Presidencial o quién sabe a quién) y ahora
todos los pasajeros se fueron y no sé si voy a caer preso
pero no: regresan con mi pasaporte al cabo de 1 hora
la CIA sabría que esta vez yo no fui a Cuba
y estuve sólo un día en el Berlín Oriental
por fin yo ya puedo pasar al registro de Aduana
sólo yo de viajero en la Aduana con mi vieja valija
y el muchacho que me registra hace como que registra
sin registrar nada y me ha dicho en voz baja "Reverendo"
y no escurca abajo en la valija donde encontraría
el disco con el último llamado de Allende al pueblo
desde La Moneda entrecortado por el ruido de las bombas
que compré en Berlín Oriental o el discurso de Fidel

The Arrival

We get off the plane and we go Nicaraguans and foreigners
scrambled together towards the large lit-up building—first
Immigration and Customs—and I am thinking as we approach
passport in hand: how proud I am, me, to be carrying
the passport of my socialist country, and the satisfaction
of arriving in a socialist Nicaragua—"Compañero . . ."
they will say to me—a revolutionary comrade made welcome
by his revolutionary comrades of Immigration and Customs
—it's not that there wouldn't be any control, there has to be
so that capitalism and Somocismo never return—
and the emotion of returning to a country in revolution
always more changes, more expropriation decrees
that they tell me about, increasingly radical transformations
many surprises during the little time one has been away
and I see joy in everyone's eyes—the ones who stayed
the others have already gone—and now we come into the light
and they ask for the passports of nationals and foreigners
but it was all a dream and I am in Somoza's Nicaragua
and they take my passport with the same cold courtesy
they would use in saying to me "come in" at Security Headquarters
and they take it inside and don't bring it back (of course
they must be phoning—of course to Security Headquarters
to the Presidential Palace or who knows where) and now
all of the passengers have gone and I don't know if I am going to be taken
                                                                    prisoner
but no: they come back with my passport at the end of an hour
the CIA would know that I didn't go to Cuba this time
and I only spent a day in East Berlin
at last I am allowed to check through Customs
the only traveler in Customs with my old bag
and the boy who searches me pretends to search
without searching anything and he has said to me softly "Reverend"
and he doesn't dig beneath in my bag where he would find
the record with Allende's final call to the people
from La Moneda broken up by the noise of the bombs
that I bought in East Germany or Fidel's speech

7

sobre el derrocamiento de Allende que me regaló Sergio
y me dice el muchacho: "Las ocho y no hemos cenado
los empleados de Aduana también sentimos hambre"
y yo: "¿A qué horas comen?" "Hasta que venga el último avión"
y ahora voy a ir hacia la tenebrosa ciudad arrasada
donde todo sigue igual y no pasa nada pero he visto
los ojos de él y me ha dicho con los ojos: "Compañero".

about the overthrow of Allende that Sergio gave me
and the boy says to me: "It's eight o'clock and we haven't eaten
we customs workers get hungry too"
and me: "What time do you eat?" "Not until after the last plane"
and now I'm going to go toward the razed and shrouded city
where everything is the same and nothing has changed but I have seen
his eyes and he has said to me with his eyes: "Compañero."

Las campesinas del Cuá

Voy a hablarles ahora de los gritos del Cuá
    gritos de mujeres como de parto
María Venancia de 90 años, sorda, casi cadáver
    grita a los guardias no he visto muchachos
la Amanda Aguilar de 50 años
        con sus hijitas Petrona y Erlinda
          no he visto muchachos
como de parto
—Tres meses en un cuartel de montaña—
Angela García de 25 y siete menores
    La Cándida de 16 años amamanta una niñita
        muy diminuta y desnutrida
Muchos han oído estos gritos del Cuá
      gemidos de la Patria como de parto
Al salir de la cárcel Estebana García con cuatro menores
dio a luz. Tuvo que regalar sus hijos
    a un finquero. Emelinda Hernández de 16
          las mejillas brillantes de llanto
    las trenzas mojadas de llanto . . .
Capturadas en Tazua cuando venían de Waslala
     la milpa en flor y ya grandes los quiquisques
     las patrullas entraban y salían con presos
       A Esteban lo montaron en el helicóptero
y al poco rato regresaron sin él . . .
       A Juan Hernández lo sacó la patrulla
una noche, y no regresó más
       Otra noche sacaron a Saturnino
y no lo volvimos a ver . . . a Chico González
      también se lo llevaron
        ésto casi cada noche
a la hora que cantan las cocorocas
gente que no conocimos también
       La Matilde abortó sentada
cuando toda una noche nos preguntaron por los guerrilleros
      A la Cándida la llamó un guardia
        vení lavame este pantalón

The Peasant Women from Cuá

Now I'll tell you about the cries from Cuá
    cries of women like pangs of birth
María Venancia, 90 years old, deaf, half dead
    shouts at the soldiers, I haven't seen any boys
Amanda Aguilar, 50 years old
        with her daughters Petrona and Erlinda
        I haven't seen any boys
like pangs of birth
—Imprisoned three months straight in a mountain barrack—
Angela García, 25 years old and seven children,
    Cándida, 16 years old, suckles a baby girl
        very tiny and underfed
Many have heard these cries from Cuá
    wails from the homeland like pangs of birth
When she left jail, Estebana García, mother of four,
gave birth to another. She had to give up her children
    to a landowner. Emelinda Hernández, 16 years old,
        her cheeks shiny with tears,
    her braids wet from crying . . .
They were captured in Tazua as they came from Waslala
    the cornfields in flower and the yucca full-grown
    the patrols came and went with prisoners
        They sent Esteban up in a helicopter
and soon after returned without him . . .
        They carried off Juan Hernández
one night, and he never came back again
        Another night they took Saturnino
and we never saw him again . . . then they took
        Chico González
        it was the same almost every night
    at the hour the *cocorocas* sing
even people we didn't know
        Matilde aborted sitting down
when they questioned her all night long about the guerrillas
    A guardsman called to Cándida
        come here and wash my pants

pero era para otra cosa
(Somoza sonreía en un retrato como un anuncio
de Alka-Seltzer)
Llegaron otros peores en un camión militar
    A los tres días que salieron parió la Cándida
Esta es la historia de los gritos del Cuá
triste como el canto de las cocorocas
la historia que cuentan las campesinas del Cuá
    que cuentan llorando
como entreviendo tras la neblina de las lágrimas una cárcel
    y sobre ella un helicóptero
    "Nosotras no sabemos de ellos"
Pero sí han visto
                sus sueños son subversivos
barbudos, borrosos en la niebla
    rápidos
        pasando un arroyo
ocultos en la milpa
        apuntando
    (como pumas)
¡saliendo de los pajonales!
pijeando a los guardias
                    viniendo al ranchito
    (sucios y gloriosos)
    la Cándida, la Amanda, la Emelinda
en sueños muchas noches
                    —con sus mochilas—
    subiendo una montaña
        con cantos de dichoso-fui
la María Venancia de 90 años
    los ven de noche en sueños
            en extrañas montañas
muchas noches
        a los muchachos.

but he wanted something else
(Somoza smiled in a picture like
an Alka-Seltzer ad)
Worse ones came in an army truck
      Three days after they left Cándida gave birth
This is the story of the cries from Cuá
sad as the *cocoroca*'s song
the story that the peasant women from Cuá tell
      that they tell in tears
as though glimpsing a jail behind the mist of tears
      and above the jail a helicopter
      "We know nothing about them"
But they have seen
                    their dreams are subversive
bearded, hazy in the mist
      quickly
        fording a stream
concealed in the cornfields
        taking aim
   (like pumas)
springing from the tall grass!
beating the guardsmen
                    coming to the farm
      (dirty and triumphant)
      Cándida, Amanda, Emelinda
so often, at night, in dreams
                    —with their knapsacks—
      climbing a mountain
      with happy-go-lucky songs
María Venancia, 90 years old,
      at night in their dreams they see the boys
              in strange mountains
so often at night in dreams
        they see the boys.

En el lago

El cielo negrísimo con todas sus estrellas
y yo mirándolas en medio lago desde una vieja lancha
    —la "María Danelia"—
acostado en la popa sobre unos sacos de arroz.
Vengo de ser interrogado por la Corte Militar
y pienso en los inmensos mundos sobre nosotros
       una sola galaxia
           (si la Tierra fuera como un grano de arroz
           la galaxia sería como la órbita de Júpiter).
Y pienso en el compañero "Modesto" en la montaña;
de origen campesino; no se sabe su nombre.
Luchan por cumplir nuestro destino en la galaxia.
Y en los campesinos colgados de las muñecas
       arrastrados de los huevos.
Un niño de 8 años degollado, dicen los Capuchinos.
Los prisioneros metidos en letrinas comunales
unos sobre otros, mujeres, niños, ancianos.
       Y esos luminosos mundos
la sociedad de las estrellas
          en torno a nosotros.
El Reino de los Cielos irradiando años-luz.
    (". . . Que os fue preparado desde el principio del mundo").
Desde que el gas primordial
salió de los negros fríos espacios inter-estelares
     y concentrándose
fue haciéndose más caliente y más brillante
       más caliente y más brillante.
¿Acaso volveremos a los espacios inter-estelares?
                Y la vida
¿no será tan característica del universo
como la luz?
        ¡Tan lejos en el espacio-tiempo!:
       Mundos que nos llegan sólo como luz.
Pero la luz no toda la vemos. En el arco-iris
tras el violeta está invisible el ultra-violeta
     Y está otro ultra tras el ultra-violeta.
     ya es la zona del amor.

On the Lake

The heavens pitch black with all their stars
and I in the middle of the lake looking at them from an old barge
   —the "María Danelia"—
lying in the stern on some sacks of rice.
I come from an interrogation at the Military Court
and I think of the immense worlds above us
      a single galaxy
         (if the Earth were like a grain of rice
         the galaxy would be like the orbit of Jupiter).
And I think of compañero "Modesto" in the mountains;
of peasant origins; no one knows his name.
They fight to fulfill our destiny in the galaxy.
And I think of the peasants hung by their wrists
      stretched by their balls.
An 8-year old's throat cut, say the Capuchin priests.
Prisoners put in communal latrines
women, children, old people piled on top of one another.
      And these luminous worlds
the society of stars
         turning around us.
The Kingdom of Heaven radiating light-years.
  (". . . that were prepared for you from the beginning of time.")
Ever since the primordial gas
came forth from the black, cold interstellar spaces
   and condensing
it grew hotter and more brilliant
      hotter and more brilliant.
Will we perhaps return to the interstellar spaces?
           And won't life
be as characteristic of the universe
as light?
     So distant in space-time!:
    Worlds that reach us only as light.
But we do not see all the light. In the rainbow
behind the violet the ultraviolet is invisible.
     And there is another ultra behind the ultraviolet
     it is already the zone of love.

Miro desde la "María Danelia" y el agua oscura de Nicaragua
           el universo de luz. La curvatura
de luz. Como volar de noche sobre Nueva York.
O mejor decir:
           las estrellas de la galaxia cogidas de la mano
           como un coro de danzantes alrededor de una hoguera
           y Pitágoras oyó las maracas.
Pero el centro de la Vía Láctea no es una estrella mayor
sino una concentración de estrellas
           (allá por la constelación del Sagitario).
Son como 1.000 mundos los que yo miro
pero los astrónomos pueden ver como un billón,
           "amar la evolución"
en Cuba escuelas, policlínicas, círculos infantiles
proliferaban como hongos después de la lluvia.
La gravedad no es sino la curvatura del universo
           esto es, su anhelo de unión.
           Tenemos un centro común y está adelante.
Muchos están presos, otros clandestinos.
A los campesinos los lanzan desde los helicópteros.
Dar la vida es entregarse al futuro.
Para ser un solo cuerpo con un solo entendimiento
y queriendo lo mismo todos juntos.
Dijo el presidente de la Corte:
           "¿Tiene usted sabido que luchan por los pobres?
           conteste sí o no".
Para cambiarse en algo más grande que uno.
Todo es movimiento: galaxia, sistema solar, planeta
con "María Danelia" la vieja lancha de los Lorío
           todo navegando por el espacio-tiempo.
           "Creo que luchan por los pobres".
Fui llamado a la Corte
y cumplí tu voluntad.
           Miro las estrellas y digo:
           he cumplido tus mandatos.
En nuestro pequeño rincón, la revolución planetaria
           una humanidad sin clases
           aquello
por lo que gira el planeta alrededor del sol.
           ¡La unificación
       del universo!
           Y las "tinieblas exteriores":
           ¿los espacios inter-estelares?
Todos es movimiento
hágase tu voluntad
así en el planeta como en las galaxias.

From the "María Danelia" and the dark water of Nicaragua I see
        the universe of light. The curvature
of light. Like flying at night over New York.
Or rather:
        the stars of the galaxy hand in hand
        like a chorus of dancers around a bonfire
            and Pythagoras heard the maracas.
But the center of the Milky Way is not a major star
but a concentration of stars
            (out there near the constellation Sagitarius).
I am looking at some 1,000 worlds
but the astronomers can see around a billion,
        "to love evolution"
in Cuba schools, polyclinics, childcare centers
proliferated like mushrooms after the rain.
Gravity is nothing but the curvature of the universe
            that is, its longing for union.
        We have a common center, and it is before us.
Many are in prison, others in the underground.
They hurl peasants from helicopters.
To give one's life is to give oneself to the future.
To be one single body with one single understanding
and loving the same thing all together.
Said the president of the Court:
        "Is it your understanding that they fight for the poor?
        Answer yes or no."
To convert oneself into something greater than one is.
All is movement: galaxy, solar system, planet
with the "María Danelia" the old barge of the Loríos
            everything navigating through space-time.
        "I believe they're struggling for the poor."
I was summoned to the Court
and I met your demand.
        I look at the stars and say:
        I have fulfilled your commands.
In our small corner, the planetary revolution
        a humanity without classes
            the end
for which the planet turns around the sun.
        The unification
    of the universe!
        And the "external darkness":
        the interstellar spaces?
All is movement
thy will be done
on earth as it is in the galaxies.

Vuelo sobre la patria sin escala

Primero fue el lago, calmo.
                    Y en él
mi lugar, lo que fue mi hogar, Solentiname.
            Todas las islas agrupadas: parecían una sola.
Pero yo podía distinguir una a una desde lejos, decir sus nombres.
La punta donde estuvo la comunidad. Todo arrasado.
La biblioteca quemada. Aquella hamaca bajo un techo de palma
                            con el lago enfrente.
Elvis y su guitarra. ¿A ellos dónde los enterró la guardia?
            Más acá La Zanata, solitaria en medio lago.
Donde íbamos a pescar guapotes.
            Casi debajo del avión pero inalcanzable.
Yo ahora vería este avión desde la hamaca de pita.
La azafata ofrece bebidas. Pido un whisky en las rocas.
Lo bebo pegada la mirada al vidrio que me separa.
Nadie en el avión sospecha esta tragedia.
                    El exilado mirando la patria.
Allí tras el vidrio.
            Pero entre yo y mi tierra hay un abismo.
Mi tierra en guerra. Fue después de lo de septiembre.
Yo volando a un congreso de la Internacional Socialista en Lisboa
a gritar por la amada azul que desde las nubes estaba viendo.
Quiero ver los lugares de las grandes manifestaciones. Los sitios
de los mítines a la luz de fogatas por las noches,
los disparos a Becats que patrullan las calles, los niños enmascarados,
las bombas de contacto, dónde es que se mueven en el monte,
las madres llorando, Monimbó, dónde arrojan a los asesinados.
Quiero. . .
            Aquello por lo que es bello morir, todo azul y nubes.
La amada geografía para mí negada.
No veía ciudades. Solo montañas azules.
                            Y de pronto
        vi Estelí,
para desgracia mía, sabía que eso era Estelí:
            Un cuadrilátero negro y negruzco
entre los campos verdes.

Flight Over the Homeland
without Stopover

First came the lake, calm.
                    And in it
my place, what was my home, Solentiname.
          All the islands grouped together: they seemed like just one.
But I could distinguish them one by one from afar, say their names.
The point where our community was. Everything demolished.
The library burned. That hammock under a roof of palms
                              with the lake in front.
Elvis and his guitar. Where did the guardsmen bury them?
          Further on, La Zanata, solitary in the middle of the lake.
Where we went to fish for *guapotes*.
          Almost right below the plane but unreachable.
I would now be seeing this plane from the fibre-thread hammock.
The stewardess offers us drinks. I ask for a whisky on the rocks.
I drink it my view glued to the window which separates me.
No one on the plane suspects this tragedy.
                    The exile looking at his homeland.
There behind the window.
                    But between me and my land there is an abyss.
My land at war. It was after the events of September.
I was flying to a congress of the Socialist International in Lisbon
to cry out for the blue beloved that I was seeing from the clouds.
I want to see the places of the large demonstrations. The sites
of the meetings by the light of campfires at night,
the shots at armored cars patrolling the streets, the masked children,
the contact bombs, where they move in the brush,
the mothers crying, Monimbó, where they throw the assassinated.
I want . . .
          That for which it is beautiful to die, all blue and clouds.
The beloved geography denied to me.
I didn't see cities. Only blue mountains.
                              And suddenly
     I saw Estelí,
to my unhappiness, I knew that this was Estelí:
          A black and murky quadrilateral
among green fields.

19

No los blancos de casitas chiquitas y colores abigarrados:
      sino una mancha de color de carbón y de ceniza
como un cuerpo carbonizado.
Nadie más ha visto nada . . . Y las azafatas
comienzan a servir la comida de plástico como que si nada.

Not the whites and motley colors of tiny houses:
      but a stain the color of coal and ash
like a burnt up corpse.
No one else has seen a thing . . . And the stewardesses
start serving plastic food as if nothing's happened.

Muchachos de "La Prensa"

Muchachos que salían a diario fotografiados en "La Prensa"
    acostados
    con los ojos entrecerrados, los labios entreabiertos
    como si se estuvieran riendo, como si estuvieran gozando.
Los jóvenes de la horrenda lista.
O bien salían serios en sus fotitos de carnet, de pasaporte,
tal vez profundamente serios.
Muchachos que aumentaban a diario la lista del horror.

Uno fue a dar una vuelta por el barrio
y lo hallaron tirado en un predio montoso.
O salió para el trabajo, de su casa del barrio San Judas,
y no volvió más.
    El que salió a comprar una Coca Cola a la esquina.
El que salió a ver a su novia y no volvió.
O sacado de su casa
    y llevado en un jeep militar que se hundió en la noche.
Y después encontrado en la morgue,
o a un lado de la carretera en la Cuesta del Plomo,
o en un basurero.
    Con los brazos quebrados,
los ojos sacados, la lengua cortada, los genitales arrancados.
    O simplemente nunca aparecieron.
Los llevados por la patrulla del "Macho Negro" o de "Cara'e León".
Los amontonados en la costa del lago detrás del Teatro Darío.

    Lo único que quedó a las mamás de sus físicos,
la mirada brillante, la sonrisa, planas, en un papel.
Cartulinas que las mamás mostraban como un tesoro en "La Prensa".
(La imagen grabada en las entrañas: en esa cartulinita chiquita).
    El del pelambre despeinado.
    El de los ojos de venado asustado.
    Este risueño, picaresco.
    La muchacha de mirada melancólica.
    Uno de perfil. O con la cabeza ladeada.
    Pensativo uno. Otro con la camisa abierta.

Kids of *La Prensa*

The boys who appeared daily in *La Prensa*
      lying down
    with eyes half-closed, lips half-opened
      as if they were laughing, as if they were enjoying it.
The young ones on the horrendous list.
Or they appeared serious in their tiny ID or passport snapshots
perhaps deeply serious.
Boys daily adding to the list of horrors.

One went for a walk through the barrio
and they found him flung on a scrubby vacant lot.
Or he left for work from his house in the San Judas barrio
and never came back.
      The one who went out to buy a Coca Cola at the corner.
The one who went out to see his girlfriend and didn't return.
Or was taken from his house
      and carried off in a military jeep that sank into the night.
And later they found him in the morgue,
or by the side of the highway on the Cuesta del Plomo,
or in a garbage dump.
      With his arms broken,
his eyes gouged out, his tongue cut out, his genitals yanked out.
      Or they simply never showed up.
Those carried off by the "Black Mule" or "Lion's Face" patrols.
Those piled up on the lakeshore behind the Darío Theater.

      The only things left for their mothers to see of their features
were their shining eyes, their smiles, flat, on a piece of paper.
Cards their mothers displayed like treasures in *La Prensa*.
(The image recorded in their guts: on these tiny cards.)
      The one with uncombed hair.
      The one with the eyes of a frightened deer.
      One smiling, roguish.
      The one with the melancholy look.
      One in profile. Or with his head turned.
      One pensive. Another with an open shirt.

Otro con bucles. O con el pelo en la cara. Con boina.
Otro borroso sonriendo debajo de sus bigotes.
Con la corbata de graduación.
La chavala sonriendo con el ceño fruncido.
La chavala en la foto que andaría su novio.
El muchacho en pose en la foto que le daría a su novia.
De 20, de 22, de 18, de 17, de 15 años.
Los jóvenes matados por ser jóvenes. Porque
tener entre los 15 y los 25 años en Nicaragua era ilegal.
        Y pareció que Nicaragua iba a quedar sin jóvenes.
Y después del triunfo hasta me sorprendí a veces, de pronto,
ante un joven que en una concentración me saludaba.
        (Yo preguntándole en mi interior: "¿Y vos cómo escapaste?").
        Se les temió por jóvenes.

Ustedes los agarrados por la guardia. Los "amados de los dioses".
Los griegos dijeron que los amados de los dioses mueren jóvenes.
Será, pienso yo, porque siempre quedaron jóvenes.
        Los otros podrán envejecer mucho pero para ellos
aquellos estarán siempre jóvenes y frescos,
        la frente tersa, el pelo negro.
La romana de pelo rubio que murió quedó siempre rubia en el recuerdo.
Pero ustedes, digo yo, no son los que no envejecieron
porque quedaron jóvenes (efímeramente) en el recuerdo
de los que también morirán.
Ustedes estarán jóvenes porque siempre habrá jóvenes en Nicaragua
y los jóvenes de Nicaragua serán ya todos revolucionarios, por
las muertes de ustedes que fueron tantos, los matados a diario.
Ellos serán ustedes otra vez, en vidas siempre renovadas,
        nuevos, como nuevo es cada amanecer.

Another with curls. Or with his hair in his face. Wearing a beret.
Another blurry, smiling under his moustache.
Wearing a necktie for graduation.
The smiling girl with a frown.
The girl in the photo her boyfriend probably carried around.
The boy posing in the photo he probably gave his girlfriend.
20, 22, 18, 17, 15 years old.
The young ones killed for being young. Because
to be between 15 and 25 years old in Nicaragua was illegal.
        And it seemed Nicaragua was going to be without the young.
And after the triumph I sometimes even was surprised, suddenly,
when a boy greeted me at a rally.
        (I asked him inwardly "And you, how did you escape?")
                They feared them because they were young.

You, the ones taken by the guards. Those "loved by the gods."
The Greeks said that those loved by the gods die young.
It's true, I think, because they stay young forever.
        Others can age a great deal but for them
those who died will always be young and fresh,
        their brows smooth, their hair black.
The Roman girl with blond hair who died always stayed blond in memories.
But you, I say, aren't the ones who didn't age
because you stayed young (ephemerally) in the memory
of those who also will die.
You will be young because there will always be youth in Nicaragua
and now Nicaragua's youth will all be revolutionaries, through
the deaths of you who were so many, the ones murdered daily.
They will be you once again, in lives ever renewed,
        new, as every dawn is new.

Barricada

Fue una tarea de todos.
Los que se fueron sin besar a su mamá
para que no supiera que se iban.
El que besó por última vez a su novia.
Y la que dejó los brazos de él para abrazar un Fal.
El que besó a la abuelita que hacía las veces de madre
y dijo que ya volvía, cogió la gorra, y no volvió.
Los que estuvieron años en la montaña. Años
en la clandestinidad, en ciudades más peligrosas que la montaña.
Los que servían de correos en los senderos sombríos del norte,
o choferes en Managua, choferes de guerrilleros cada anochecer.
Los que compraban armas en el extranjero tratando con gangsters.
Los que montaban mítines en el extranjero con banderas y gritos
o pisaban la alfombra de la sala de audiencias de un presidente.
Los que asaltaban cuarteles al grito de Patria Libre o Morir.
El muchacho vigilante en la esquina de la calle liberada
con un pañuelo roji-negro en el rostro.
Los niños acarreando adoquines,
        arrancando los adoquines de las calles
           —que fueron un negocio de Somoza—
y acarreando adoquines y adoquines
        para las barricadas del pueblo.
Las que llevaban café a los muchachos que estaban en las barricadas.
Los que hicieron las tareas importantes,
        y los que hacían las menos importantes:
Esto fue una tarea de todos.
La verdad es que todos pusimos adoquines en la gran barricada.
Fue una tarea de todos. Fue el pueblo unido.
        Y lo hicimos.

Barricade

It was everybody's task.
The ones who went off without kissing their mothers
so they wouldn't know they'd left.
The boy who kissed his girlfriend for the last time.
And the girl who left her boyfriend's arms to embrace a Fal.
The one who kissed his grandmother who was like a mother to him
and said he'd come back soon, took his cap, and didn't return.
Those who were in the mountains for years. Years
in the underground, in cities more dangerous than the mountains.
The ones who served as couriers along the shady paths of the north,
or as chauffeurs in Managua, chauffeurs of guerrillas every dusk.
Those who bought arms abroad dealing with gangsters.
Those who set up meetings abroad with flags and shouts
or walked the rugs of a president's reception room.
Those who assaulted barracks with the cry of Free Homeland or Death.
The vigilant boy on the corner of the liberated street
with a red and black kerchief over his face.
The children carting streetstones,
            yanking them from the streets
                  —the stones a business for Somoza—
and carting streetstones and streetstones
                  for the people's barricades.
The women who brought coffee to the kids along the barricades.
Those who did the important jobs,
                  and those who did the less important ones.
This was everybody's task.
The truth is that all of us put streetstones in the great barricade.
It was everybody's task. It was the people united.
                  And we did it.

II

VUELOS DE VICTORIA Y CELEBRACIÓN
FLIGHTS OF VICTORY AND CELEBRATION

Luces

Aquel vuelo clandestino de noche.
Con peligro de ser derribados. La noche serena.
El cielo lleno, llenísimo de estrellas. La Vía Láctea
clarísima tras el grueso vidrio de la ventanilla,
    masa blancuzca y rutilante en la noche negra
con sus millones de procesos de evoluciones y revoluciones.
Íbamos sobre el mar para evitar la aviación somocista,
    pero cerca de la costa.
El pequeño avión volando bajo, y volando lento.
Primero las luces de Rivas, tomada y retomada por los Sandinistas,
    ahora a medias en poder de los Sandinistas.
Después otras luces: Granada, en poder de la guardia
    (sería atacada esa noche).
Masaya, totalmente liberada. Tantos cayeron allí.
Más allá un resplandor: Managua. Lugar de tantos combates.
(El Bunker—todavía el bastión de la guardia).
Diriamba, liberada. Jinotepe, con combates. Tanto heroísmo
relumbra en esas luces. Montelimar—nos señalaba el piloto—:
la hacienda del tirano junto al mar. Al lado, Puerto Somoza.
La Vía Láctea arriba, y las luces de la revolución de Nicaragua.
Me parece mirar más lejos, en el norte, la fogata de Sandino
    ("Aquella luz es Sandino").
Las estrellas sobre nosotros, y la pequeñez de esta tierra
pero también la importancia de ella, de estas
pequeñitas luces de los hombres. Pienso: todo es luz.
El planeta viene del sol. Es luz hecha sólida.
La electricidad de este avión es luz. El metal es luz. El calor
    de la vida viene del sol.
    "Hágase la luz".
También están las tinieblas.
Hay extraños reflejos—no sé de donde vienen—en
    la superficie transparente de la ventanilla.
Una luminosidad roja: las luces de la cola del avión.
Y reflejos en el mar tranquilo: serán las estrellas.
Miro la lucecita de mi cigarrillo—también viene del sol,
    de una estrella.

Lights

That clandestine night flight.
Running the risk of being shot down. The night serene.
The heavens filled, so filled with stars. The Milky Way
so clear beyond the thick glass of the window,
            a whitish and shimmering mass in the black night
with its millions of processes of evolutions and revolutions.
We were flying over the sea to evade the Somoza airforce,
            but near the coast.
The little plane flying low, and flying slow.
First the lights of Rivas, taken and retaken by the Sandinistas,
            now halfway in the Sandinistas' hands.
Then other lights: Granada, in the hands of the guard
                    (it would be attacked that night).
Masaya, completely liberated. So many fell there.
Further on, a glitter: Managua. The site of so many battles.
(The Bunker—still the bastion of the guard.)
Diriamba: liberated. Jinotepe, still fighting. So much heroism
shines in those lights. Montelimar—the pilot points it out—:
the tyrant's seaside estate. Beside it Puerto Somoza.
The Milky Way above, and the lights of Nicaragua's revolution.
I seem to see further off, in the north, Sandino's campfire
                    ("That light is Sandino").
The stars above us, and the smallness of this earth
but the importance of it as well, of these
tiny little human lights. I think: everything is light.
The planet comes from the sun. It is light made solid.
This plane's electricity is light. The metal is light. Life's
                    warmth comes from the sun.
                    "Let there be light."
There is darkness too.
There are strange reflections—I don't know where they come from—on
                    the clear surface of the windows.
A red luminosity: the plane's taillights.
And reflections on the calm sea: they must be the stars.
I look at my cigarette's glow—it too comes from the sun,
                    from a star.

31

Y la silueta de un barco grande. ¿El portavión de los EE. UU.
enviado a patrullar la costa del Pacífico?
Una gran luz a la derecha nos sobresalta. ¿Un jet contra nosotros?
No. La luna que sale, media luna, serenísima, iluminada por el sol.
    El peligro de ir volando en una noche tan clara.
Y el radio de pronto. Palabras confusas llenando el pequeño avión.
¿La guardia? El piloto dice: "son los nuestros".
        Esas ondas son de nosotros.
Ya estamos cerca de León, el territorio liberado.
Una intensa luz rojo-anaranjada, como la brasa de un puro: Corinto:
la potente iluminación de los muelles rielando en el mar.
Y ahora ya la playa de Poneloya, y el avión entrando a tierra,
el cordón de espuma de la costa radiante bajo la luna.
        El avión bajando. Un olor a insecticida.
Y me dice Sergio: "¡El olor de Nicaragua!"
Es el momento de mayor peligro, la aviación enemiga
        puede estar esperándonos sobre este aeropuerto.
Y ya las luces del aeropuerto.
Estamos en tierra. Salen de la oscuridad los compas verde-olivo a

                                                    abrazarnos.
Sentimos sus cuerpos calientes, que también vienen del sol,
que también son luz.
        Es contra las tinieblas esta revolución.
Era la madrugada del 18 de julio. Y el comienzo
        de todo lo que estaba por venir.

And the silhouette of a big ship. The U.S. aircraft carrier
sent to patrol the Pacific coast?
A big light on the right startles us. A jet against us?
No. The moon coming up, a halfmoon, so serene, lit by the sun.
      The danger of flying on such a clear night.
And suddenly the radio. Confused words filling the little plane.
The guard? The pilot says: "they're ours."
      Those waves are ours.
Now we're near León, liberated territory.
An intense reddish-orange light, like the red-hot glow of a cigar: Corinto:
the powerful dock lights shimmering on the sea.
And now the Poneloya beach, and the plane coming in to land,
the coast a line of foam radiating light beneath the moon.
      The plane descending. A smell of insecticide.
And Sergio says to me: "The smell of Nicaragua!"
This is the most dangerous part, the enemy airforce
      could be waiting for us over this airport.
And finally the airport lights.
We've landed. Comrades clad in olive-green come out of the dark
                                          to embrace us.
We feel their warm bodies, which also come from the sun,
which are also light.
      It's against the darkness, this revolution.
It was the dawn of July 18. And the beginning
      of everything that was to come.

Meditación en un DC-3

No sé por qué recordé la frase de Novalis
"Tocar un cuerpo desnudo es tocar el cielo".
El piloto militar abría el mapa de la patria
      para la niña morena de nueve años
(abajo la tierra nuestra)
su mano rozando su manita.
Abajo Muy-Muy, ríos, Nueva Guinea donde cayó Felipe.
     "Es tocar el cielo . . ."
            ¿Pero si no creen en el cielo?
Es claro que no es la bóveda azul atmosférica
      eso es siempre la tierra
y el ir volando en un DC-3 en el cielo de la patria liberada
es la tierra.
Pero la infinita noche negra
de las estrellas, con nuestra Tierra llena de humanos que se aman
     y todas las demás amorosas Tierras
                es el cielo
       es el Reino de los Cielos.
¿Y Novalis qué quiso decir?
     Para mí está diciendo:
besuquear un bebé,
pareja con caricias profundas,
apretón de manos,
palmadita en el hombro,
lo humano tocando lo humano,
la unión de piel humana con piel humana
es tocar el Comunismo con el dedo compañeros.

Meditation in a DC-3

I don't know why I recalled the words of Novalis:
"Touching a naked body is touching heaven."
The military pilot opened the map of the homeland
      for the dark-skinned girl of nine
(below, our land)
his hand touching her small hand.
Below was Muy-Muy, rivers, Nuevo Guinea where Felipe fell.
        "Is touching heaven . . ."
            But if they don't believe in heaven?
It's clear it's not the blue atmospheric vault
      it's still the earth
and to go flying in a DC-3 in the sky of the liberated homeland
is the earth.
But the infinite black night
of the stars, with our Earth full of humans who love each other
      and all the other loving Earths
                is heaven
        it's the Kingdom of Heaven.
And what did Novalis mean to say?
      For me he's saying:
kissing a baby,
a couple in deep embrace,
squeezing hands,
a tiny palm on the shoulder,
human being touching human being,
the union of human skin with human skin
is touching Communism with your finger, compañeros.

Aterrizaje con epitafio

El gran avión va sobre las nubes sonrosadas
del amanecer,
        en el Atlántico, y después el Caribe,
siempre en la dirección del sol, y siempre
en el amanecer,
y ahora la tierra,
        las montañas liberadas de Nicaragua
        las montañas recién alfabetizadas
y siempre las nubes sonrosadas, siempre en el amanecer
y luego bajando hacia el aeropuerto
y ya vamos a tocar tierra
        y al mirar de cerca la tierra
pienso, no sé por qué, en los muertos,
no todos, sino *ellos,*
        nuestros muertos,
en las montañas, en zanjas comunes, en tumba solitaria,
en cementerios, a la vera de caminos,
cerca de este aeropuerto, por todo el territorio nacional,
con monumentos, anónimos sin ningún monumento,
todos hechos esta tierra, haciendo más sagrada esta tierra,
Sandino, Carlos Fonseca, Julio Buitrago, Oscar Turcios,
Ricardo Morales Avilés, Rugama, Eduardo Contreras,
Carlos Agüero, Claudia Chamorro, Luisa Amanda Espinosa,
Luis Alfonso Velázquez, Arlen Siú, Ernesto Castillo,
Pedro Joaquín, José Benito Escobar, David Tejada,
Pomares, Silvio Mayorga, Rigoberto, Pablo Ubeda, Gaspar
el Chato Medrano, Donald y Elvis, Felipe Peña,
y tantos más, y tantos más, y tantos más:
Que me entierren en esta tierra junto con ustedes Compañeros
     Muertos.
Las ruedas ya a pocos metros de la tierra.
Y debiera decir una voz en el micrófono: Señoras y Señores
la tierra que vamos a tocar es muy sagrada.
. . . Las ruedas ya acaban de tocar, señores pasajeros,
una gran tumba de mártires.

Landing with Epitaph

The great plane flies over the pinkened clouds
of dawn,
          over the Atlantic, and then over the Caribbean,
always in the direction of the sun, and always
at dawn,
and now the land,
               the liberated mountains of Nicaragua
                    the recently "literated" mountains
and always the pinkened clouds, always at dawn
and then heading down toward the airport
and now we're going to touch down
                    and seeing the ground up close
I think, I don't know why, of the dead ones,
not all of them, but *those,*
               our dead ones,
in the mountains, in common ditches, in a solitary tomb,
in cemeteries, on the roadsides,
near this airport, all over the country,
the ones with monuments, the anonymous ones without any monument,
all transformed into this soil, making this soil more sacred,
Sandino, Carlos Fonseca, Julio Buitrago, Oscar Turcios,
Ricardo Morales Avilés, Rugama, Eduardo Contreras,
Carlos Agüero, Claudia Chamorro, Luisa Amanda Espinosa,
Luis Alfonso Velázquez, Arlen Siú, Ernesto Castillo,
Pedro Joaquín, José Benito Escobar, David Tejada,
Pomares, Silvio Mayorga, Rigoberto, Pablo Ubeda, Gaspar
el Chato Medrano, Donald and Elvis, Felipe Peña,
and so many more, and so many more, and so many more:
May I be buried in this soil together with you Comrades,
          Death's Comrades.
The wheels now only a few meters off the ground.
And a voice over the microphone should say: Ladies and Gentlemen
the ground we're about to touch is very sacred.
. . . The wheels have just landed, passengers,
on a great tomb of martyrs.

37

Otra llegada

Fue a la semana después del triunfo.
Veníamos de Cuba
            de la celebración del 26 de julio.
Yo iba recordando el discurso de Fidel
y la frase de Martí, "Todo es gloria en julio".
Y aparece de pronto, azul sobre el azul, el Momotombo
libre por primera vez desde la época de los indios.
Los campos cuadriculados, de dulces verdes, al amanecer.
            El lago de Managua sonrosado en ese amanecer,
la pequeña Isla del Pájaro junto a Managua
(también era de Somoza,
el primer Somoza le quiso cambiar el nombre por Isla del Amor)
y me doy cuenta que se ve ahora *más bello* el país.
Y se lo digo a Dora María que va a mi lado
mirando también extasiada la patria liberada
este sueño que todos estamos viviendo y del que jamás despertaremos.
            Antes esta belleza estaba como abochornada . . .
Qué bello se ve ahora el país.
            Qué hermosa ahora nuestra naturaleza sin Somoza.
Y la emoción de oir sobre el lago rosicler
a la azafata de Cubana de Aviación anunciar
que vamos a aterrizar en el aeropuerto "Augusto César Sandino".
            El avión lleno de comandantes guerrilleros.
Y ahora el bajarse sin temor
            (y por cierto que no andábamos pasaporte)
y llegar a Migración, y llegar a Aduana,
y que le digan a uno: "Compañero".

Another Arrival

It was a week after the triumph.
We were coming from Cuba
        from the July 26 celebration.
I kept remembering Fidel's speech
and the phrase from Martí, "All is glory in July."
And all at once, blue on blue, Momotombo
free for the first time since the epoch of the Indians.
The squared off fields of sweet greens at dawn.
        Lake Managua blushing in this dawn,
the small Isla del Pájaro next to Managua
(it too belonged to Somoza,
the first Somoza wanted to change its name to Isla del Amor)
and I realize that the country looks *more beautiful.*
And I say this to Dora María who sits at my side
also looking ecstatically at the liberated homeland
this dream which we're all living and from which we'll never awaken.
        Before this beauty was as if ashamed of itself . . .
How beautiful the country looks now.
        How lovely our nature now without Somoza.
And our excitement as we hear over the dawn-pink lake
the Cuban Airlines stewardess announce
that we're going to land at the "Augusto César Sandino Airport."
        The plane filled with guerrilla commanders.
And now getting off without fear
        (and we didn't even have passports)
and arriving at Immigration, and arriving at Customs,
and them saying to each of us: "Compañero."

Visión de un rostro

Sol y banderas,
            primero los himnos,
   sol y consignas,
               pancartas y parlantes,
aplausos y consignas,
           sol y sonrisas,
ojos de todos los colores,
      todo tono de piel,
         toda clase de pelo,
cada boca sonriente distinta, cada nariz diferente
(los ojos: luz de innumerables colores enmarcados en blanco),
pelo largo, corto, liso, ensortijado, afro,
jóvenes, el gordo, mujer con un niñito, ancianita arrugada, chavalitos,
pantalón amarillo, blusa roja, camiseta blanca, rojo, azul,
blanco, verde-olivo, negro, anaranjado, rosado, amarillo.
Y vi de pronto desde la tribuna un solo rostro
con millares de sonrisas y millares de pares de ojos,
un Rostro de rostros, un Cuerpo de cuerpos,
como esas fotos de los periódicos de puntitos y puntitos.
        Rostro borroso todavía, pero tenía como una aureola . . .
(¿O un sombrero aludo, o una boina?).
Vi que esa carne unida era el triunfo sobre la muerte.
Los fotógrafos lanzando sus flashs. La gente apretujándose,
       y se veía la unidad de todos,
la unidad garantía de la Victoria.

Vision of a Face

Sun and flags,
        first the hymns,
   sun and rallying cries,
         signs and loudspeakers,
applause and rallying cries,
        sun and smiles,
eyes of every color,
      every tone of skin,
       every kind of hair,
each smiling mouth distinct, each nose different
(eyes: light from countless colors framed in white),
long, short, straight, curly, afro hair,
young people, a fat man, a woman with a small child, an old wrinkled
                                      woman, little kids,
yellow pants, red blouse, white T-shirt, red, blue,
white, olive-green of the uniforms, black, orange, pink, yellow.
And suddenly from the stand I saw one face
with thousands of smiles and thousands of pairs of eyes,
a Face of faces, a Body of bodies,
like those newspaper photos made up of tiny dots.
       The face was still blurry, but it had a kind of halo . . .
(A wide-brimmed hat or a beret?)
I saw that this united flesh was the victory over death.
Photographers flashing away. The people squeezing together,
       and you could see the unity of everyone,
unity the guarantee of Victory.

La mano

En el concurso de carrozas revolucionarias
            —yo uno de los jurados
                en una tribuna, al lado
del Comandante Tomás, viendo
pasar las carrozas, y el río de gente
la mayoría saludando, las manos levantadas,
                las palmas agitadas,
                    o bien puños cerrados:
        de pronto vi
                    una mano.
Borrado todo lo demás vi sólo esa mano levantada
como cuando la cámara se acerca para enfocar sólo un detalle
una palma y los cinco dedos separados.
¿Y qué me decía esa mano?
Me mostraba el órgano más humano de lo humano
aquello por lo que pasamos del mono a humanos
y el más perfecto miembro del cuerpo humano.
¿Lo desarrollamos agarrándonos de las ramas?
Un espacio plano con cinco prolongaciones cilíndricas ágiles
como acróbatas.
                La mano saludaba.
Aquello que labró el primer pedernal
lo que hizo rascacielos, libros, telas, tractores y violines
y también estas carrozas,
una palma y cinco dedos,
lo que hizo que el homínido pensara y hablara,
descubriera el fuego,
hiciera estas carrozas revolucionarias,
hiciera una Revolución.
La mano que también empuñó el arma en las barricadas,
alzó hacia el cielo el fusil de silueta estilizada.
                Todo lo que es hecho,
todo lo humano de la tierra es hecho por manos.
No pude saber si era mano de hombre o mujer
pero era mano para estrechar otras manos, o
                otra mano,

42

The Hand

In the contest of revolutionary floats
      —I was one of the judges
          in a jury, seated next to
Commander Tomás, watching
the floats pass by, and the river of people
most of them saluting, hands raised,
        palms waving,
          or fists clenched:
    suddenly I saw
        a hand.
Everything else blurred, I saw only this raised hand
like when a camera closes in to focus on a single detail
a palm and five separate fingers.
And what did this hand say to me?
It showed me the most human of human organs
the organ by which we went from monkey to human
and the most perfect member of the human body.
Did we develop it clutching at branches?
A flat space with five cylindrical prolongations agile
as acrobats.
        The hand saluted.
That hand which fashioned the first flint
which made skyscrapers, books, fabrics, tractors, and violins
and these floats as well,
a palm and five fingers,
which made primal man think and speak,
discover fire,
make these revolutionary floats,
make a Revolution.
The hand too which clutched a weapon on the barricades,
raised a rifle toward the sky in a stylized silhouette.
      All that is made,
everything human on earth is made by hands.
I couldn't tell if it was the hand of a man or woman
but it was a hand to grasp other hands, or
        another hand,

43

y para acariciar también otro ser humano.
Nada más humano que una mano
hermano dame tu mano
también se nos dio las manos hermano para ir juntos de la mano
mano a mano
de la mano.
Y se fue esa mano
y más manos levantadas van saludando . . .

to caress another human being.
           Nothing more human than a hand
                brother give me your hand
hands were also given to us, brother, to go hands joined to hands
           hand in hand
                by the hand.
And this hand went away
and more raised hands go on saluting . . .

Llegaron las del Cuá

Y también llegaron al gran acto de masas las del Cuá.
La mujer de Jacinto Hernández caído en Kuskawás.
La mujer de Bernardino.
                    La Amanda Aguilar.
Una delegación del Cuá.
            También vinieron con niños.
Recordaron los dolores, los "Sucesos del Cuá".
Del Cuá que no decía dónde estaban los guerrilleros.
            Amanda Aguilar conocía un poema sobre el Cuá.
(Amanda Aguilar era seudónimo, su nombre es Petrona Hernández).
Eran llevadas junto con los niños al comando del Cuá.
            "Algunas estábamos embarazadas".
Quedaron sin sus casas.
Angelina Díaz dijo:
            "Íbamos por la montaña de un lugar a otro".
Y la viuda de Bernardino:
            "Golpeado y sucio, vendado, se lo llevaron".
Una historia que no se olvida, dijo Juana Tinoco.
Contó de las torturas a los niñitos.
        Los niñitos gritando en aquel comando.
            "Era para que dijeran quiénes dábamos de comer".
Y la viuda de Bernardino:
"El tenía un hijo enfermo, y lo consolaba en el tabanco.
Llegó la guardia. Y le gritaron que se bajara.
        El dijo: ¡Estoy contumeriando a mi hijo!
El teniente me dijo:
            Despedite de tu maridito que no lo volverás a ver.
Yo me fuí caminando detrás de él".
Bernardino Díaz Ochoa, el que dijo:
            "No somos aves para vivir del aire,
            no somos peces para vivir del mar,
            somos hombres para vivir de la tierra".
Cuando se llevaron a Bernardino era el tiempo de los elotes.
Y también contó la mujer de Bernardino:
"Le sacaron la lengua con un tortol.
Le metieron clavos en los oídos.

46

The Women from Cuá Arrived

And the women from Cuá also came to the great mass rally.
The wife of Jacinto Hernández who fell at Kuskawás.
The wife of Bernardino.
                                    Amanda Aguilar.
A delegation from Cuá.
                       They came with children also.
They recalled their sorrows, the "Events at Cuá."
At the Cuá which never told where the guerrillas were.
                Amanda Aguilar knew a poem about Cuá.
(Amanda Aguilar was a pseudonym, her name is Petrona Hernández.)
They were taken with their children to the command post of Cuá.
               "Some of us were pregnant."
They were left homeless.
Angelina Díaz said:
               "We went from place to place through the countryside."
And Bernardino's widow:
               "Battered and dirty, blindfolded, they carried him off."
A story one can never forget, said Juana Tinoco.
She told of the tortures to their little children.
            Their little children screaming in that command post.
             "It was so they'd tell who we were giving food to."
And Bernardino's widow:
"He had a sick son, and was comforting him in our little loft.
The guards arrived. And they yelled that he should come down.
            He said: I'm just tending to my son!
The lieutenant told me:
            Say good-bye to that husband of yours, you'll never see him again.
I went following after him."
Bernardino Díaz Ochoa, the one who said:
            "We're not birds meant to live off the air,
            we're not fish meant to live off the sea,
            we're men meant to live off the earth."
When they took Bernardino away it was cornhusking time.
And Bernardino's wife also recounted:
"They pulled out his tongue with a barnacle clamp.
They stuck nails in his ears.

Le preguntaban: ¿Cuántos guerrilleros pasan? ¿Conocés a Tomás Borge?
Cuando lo mataron, los guardias estaban bebiendo cususa''.
       Día y noche allí siempre fue de noche.
Hasta que triunfó la revolución de los muchachos.
Entonces fue como que les quitaran una capucha.
La Amanda Aguilar les llevaba comida a los guerrilleros.
       Estas cosas contaron las del Cuá.
Llegaron vestidas humildemente
con un cartel que decía: ¡Las Mujeres del Cuá, Presente!
       Esta fue la noticia periodística
de la llegada de la delegación de las campesinas del Cuá.

They'd asked him: How many guerrillas come here? Do you know Tomás
                                                                    Borge?
When they killed him, the guardsmen were drinking raw booze.''
          There day and night were always night.
Until the revolution of the boys triumphed.
Then it was as if they pulled off their hoods.
Amanda Aguilar brought food to the guerrillas.
          These things the ones from Cuá related.
Humbly dressed they came
with a placard that read: The women of Cuá, Present!
          This was the journalistic report
about the arrival of the delegation of peasant women from Cuá.

Libres

Comandante, cuando estábamos
              con la Asociación de Niños Sandinistas
y vos dijiste una frase de tu discurso,
una frase sencilla
        "ahora somos libres"
                (concatenada a otras frases)
yo ví en el momento preciso de esa frase
el movimiento de unos niños en las graderías,
unos subiendo y otro, chiquito, trabajosamente bajando,
              uno comiéndose un helado,
había mucho movimiento y aún desorden en la alegre
                        aglomeración
              de niños y jovencitos
bajo la voz magnificada por los micrófonos y su gran eco,
y sentí que todos esos niños eran libres, y lo sabían,
el de 7 años chupando su helado, libre para siempre,
crecerán libres,
como el compa que me dijo cuando íbamos en la carretera
que creyó que nunca podría andar en carro
              en una carretera
        como veía desde el monte pasar a la guardia,
              a los de la EEBI,
que siempre andaría clandestino o en el monte;
o como el campesino de El Jocote, adelante de Palacagüina,
que dijo que ya iba a las fiestas de noche sin temor,
sin temor a aquel helicóptero que se llevaba
                  a los campesinos
              y ya no volvían,
que antes se sentía como un pájaro enjaulado:
todo esto ví rápido en una visión cuando dijiste esa frase,
y ya seguías diciendo otras frases, Comandante.

Free

Commander, when we were
                at the Association of Sandinista Children
and you uttered a phrase in your speech,
a simple phrase
        "now we are free"
           (linked with other phrases)
at the very moment you uttered this phrase I saw
the movement of some children in the grandstand,
some climbing up and another, a tot, laboriously clambering down,
           another eating an ice cream,
there was plenty of movement and even disorder in the joyous
           conglomeration
        of children and young ones
under your booming and echoing voice magnified by microphones,
and I felt that all these children were free, and they knew it,
the 7-year old sucking on his ice cream, free forevermore,
they will grow up free,
like the young soldier who told me as we drove along the highway
that he had believed he would never be able to drive
        on a highway
      that from the woods as he watched the guards
        and the secret police go by,
he thought he would always be underground or in the woods;
or like the peasant from El Jocote, beyond Palacagüina,
who said that now he went to the nighttime fiestas unafraid,
unafraid of that helicopter that carried off
          the peasants
        and they never came back,
that before he had felt like a caged bird:
all this I saw flash in a vision when you pronounced this phrase,
and you were already saying other phrases, Commander.

La mañanita

Hermano, amaneció. Mirá.
Ahora podemos ver ya el volcán Masaya
                    y su humo
saliendo del cráter, y la laguna, verde, de Masaya,
más allá la laguna de Apoyo, muy azul,
las Sierras, y serranías de color cielo
                  hasta la lejanía, la verdad es
            que nuestra tierra es de color de cielo,
más lejos, ¿lo ves? el Pacífico,
             casi puro cielo bajo el cielo,
la verdad es que estamos en el cielo y no lo sabemos,
mirá, del otro lado el lago de Managua y el Momotombo
                    junto al agua como
        un triángulo de lago levantado o
             una pirámide de cielo.
Todo esto desde antes estaba allí
          pero una oscura noche lo cubría,
y no se veía. La noche de las tentaciones.
          Cada uno tenía su tentación.
La tentación del falso amanecer que aún no podía ser.
El yacer en una cama en plena noche soñando que es el amanecer.
Ahora sí fue el amanecer, Pancho Nicaragua,
          todo está iluminado
alrededor de este rancho.
        La tierra y el agua. Lo podés ver.
Y en aquella casita oigo cantar:
          "Qué alegre y fresca
          la mañanita".

The Morning

Brother, dawn has come. Look.
Now we can already see the Masaya Volcano
      and its smoke
rising from the crater, and the Masaya Lagoon, green,
further on, the Apoyo Lagoon, very blue,
the Sierra Mountains and the mountain ranges, sky-blue
     out to the distance, the truth is
   that our land is sky-blue,
still further on, you see it? The Pacific,
     almost pure blue under the sky,
the truth is that we're in heaven and don't know it,
look, on the other side of Lake Managua and Momotombo
       next to the water like
   a risen triangle of lake or
    a pyramid of sky.
All this was here before
    but a dark night covered it,
and you couldn't see it. The night of temptations.
     Each one of us had our temptation.
The temptation of a false dawn that still couldn't be.
Lying in bed in darkest night dreaming it's dawn.
Now yes, dawn's come, Pancho Nicaragua,
    everything is lit up
around this hut.
    Earth and water. You can see it.
And in that little house I hear them sing:
      "How joyous and fresh
     is the new morning."

III

VUELOS DE RECONSTRUCCIÓN
FLIGHTS OF RECONSTRUCTION

Ocupados

Estamos todos muy ocupados
la verdad es que estamos todos tan ocupados
en estos días difíciles y jubilosos, que no volverán
                    pero que nunca olvidaremos
estamos muy ocupados con las confiscaciones
              tantas confiscaciones
tantas reparticiones de tierras
quitando todo mundo las barricadas de las calles
            para que puedan pasar los carros
      las barricadas de todos los barrios
también cambiando nombres de calles y de barrios
              aquellos nombres somocistas
desenterrando a los asesinados
reparando los hospitales bombardeados
       —este hospital se llamará tal y tal—
creando ya la nueva policía
censando a los artistas
llevando el agua potable a tal o cual lugar
y estos otros están pidiendo la luz eléctrica
          la luz que el dictador les había cortado
rápido, rápido restaurar las instalaciones
        agua y luz para Ciudad Sandino
    —ellos decidieron llamar su barrio Ciudad Sandino—
estamos muy ocupados, Carlos
los mercados deben estar limpios, deben estar bien ordenados
        hay que hacer también más mercados
estamos creando nuevos parques, claro y ya nuevas leyes
      rápido prohibimos los anuncios pornográficos
los precios de granos básicos bien controlados
es tiempo de hacer también muchos afiches
rápido, rápido hay que nombrar nuevos jueces
rápido reparar las carreteras
y qué bello, también hay que trazar nuevas carreteras
elección de juntas de gobiernos locales
es hora de que un millón aprenderán a leer
vos vas a tu reunión de gabinete, vos vas a tu sindicato

Busy

We're all very busy
the truth is that we're all so busy
in these difficult and jubilant days, that will never come back
                                    but we will never forget
we're very busy with the confiscations
                    so many confiscations
so many land distributions
everyone taking down the street barricades
                    so the cars can get through
          the barricades in all the neighborhoods
changing the names of the streets and neighborhoods as well
                    those Somocista names
digging up the murdered ones
repairing the bombarded hospitals
          —this hospital will be called such and such—
now creating the new police force
doing a count of the artists
bringing drinking water to one place or another
and still others are asking for electric light
               the light the dictator had cut off
quickly, quickly restoring the installations
              water and light for Sandino City
          —they decided to call their neighborhood Sandino City—
we're very busy, Carlos
the markets should be clean, they should be well ordered
             we also have to build more markets
we're creating new parks, of course, and new laws too
          right off we prohibit pornographic ads
basic grain prices well controlled
it's also time to make lots of posters
quickly, quickly we have to name new judges
quickly repair the highways
and how beautiful, we have to design new highways
the election of local governmental councils
it's time for a million to learn to read
you go to your cabinet meeting, you go to your union

la vacunación a los niños de todo el país
y ya mismo los planes de educación
las palas mecánicas limpiando los escombros
       —Monimbó otra vez con marimbas—
los campos rumoreando de tractores
organizada ya la asociación de trabajadores del campo
semillas, insecticidas, abonos, nueva conciencia
y rápido, hay que sembrar muy rápido
también es el tiempo de nuevos cantos
los obreros volvieron a sus ruidosas ruedas con alegría
hermano, se restablecieron todas las rutas de buses urbanos
      —y tantos festivales culturales en los barrios
        actos político-culturales ahora les llaman—
y también todos los días son las misas de los compañeros caídos
y hay una palabra nueva en nuestro hablar cotidiano
                         "Compañero"
todo esto quedará para quien quiera verlo en los viejos periódicos
en periódicos amarillos el comienzo de la nueva historia
        periódicos poéticos
allí verán en hermosos titulares lo que yo ahora digo
de estos días embriagantes que no volverán
de estos días en que estamos tan ocupados
porque la verdad es que estamos muy ocupados.

the vaccination of children throughout the country
and right now the plans for education
the mechanical shovels cleaning up the ruins
                    —Monimbó once more with marimbas—
the fields humming with tractors
the field workers' association already organized
seeds, insecticides, fertilizers, new consciousness
and quickly, we have to plant very quickly
it's also the time for new songs
the workers have returned to their noisy wheels with joy
brother, they've reestablished all the urban bus routes
                    —and so many cultural festivals in the neighborhoods
                    now they call them cultural-political acts—
and then too the masses they hold daily for the fallen compañeros
and there's a new word in our everyday speech
                                        "Compañero"
all this will remain for whoever wishes to see it in old newspapers
in yellowing newspapers the beginning of the new history
                    poetic newspapers
there in lovely headlines they'll see what I now say
of these intoxicating days that will never return
of these days when we're so busy
because the truth is that we're very busy.

Reflexiones de un ministro

Qué se va a hacer. Soy Ministro de Cultura,
y voy a una recepción a la embajada tal.
¿Cuál? Para qué decir cuál.
Tal o cual, es igual.
Y de pronto junto a la cuneta, entre el pasto
          un gato.
Las dos luces del carro prenden las dos del gato.
Quisiera quedarme aquí
         para observar mejor este gato,
            de qué color es,
(de noche dice el dicho todos son del mismo color),
         qué iba a hacer después, cómo
su lomo se iba a mover.
Quedarme junto a la cuneta con el gato
                      mi gato
fuera mejor
         aunque sea un imitador de Marianne Moore
—por ejemplo aquel su gato con un ratón en la boca
la cola colgándole como un cordón de zapato.
Dice Davenport de Marianne Moore: "el poeta
está más interesado en la avestruz
         que el ornitologista
            que escribió *Avestruz*
en la *Enciclopedia Británica*".
Yo voy pensando en el gato y Marianne Moore.
         No more:
ya he entrado a la embajada iluminada
         y saludo al Señor Embajador.

Reflections of a Minister

What can you do. I'm the Minister of Culture,
and I go to the reception of some embassy.
Which one? Why say which.
One or another, it's all the same thing.
And suddenly next to the curb, in the grass
        a cat.
The car's two lights light up the cat's two.
I'd like to stay here
      to observe this cat all the more,
         what his color is,
(at night, goes the saying, they're all the same color),
        what he'd be up to later, how
his back would arch.
Staying next to the curb with the cat
              my cat
would be better
        even if that makes me a Marianne Moore copycat
—for instance that cat of hers with a mouse in its mouth
the mouse tail dangling like a shoestring.
Davenport says of Marianne Moore: "the poet shows more
interest in the ostrich
        than the ornithologist
           who wrote the ostrich entry for
the *Encyclopaedia Britannica.*"
I go off musing on the cat and Marianne Moore.
        No more:
now I'm entering the lit up embassy
        and I'm greeting Mr. Ambassador.

Reunión del gabinete

Citados para una reunión de gabinete,
de antemano sabiendo que por una razón muy importante
pero no cuál.
Todos los ministros y directores de entes auntónomos
      en la gran mesa.
Y era una cuestión grave:
La integración de un Comité de Emergencia Nacional
por el peligro de plaga del mosquito *Aedes aegypti.*
Se cría especialmente en recipientes artificiales.
      Puede reconocerse por sus líneas plateadas en el tórax.
Es la hembra la que pica al ser humano.
Necesita la sangre para sus huevos
que deposita en cualquier recipiente con agua.
Hay que hacer la campaña preventiva en
floreros, envases, llantas viejas, barriles, canales del techo,
      la eliminación de objetos inservibles,
         limpieza en los patios,
            fumigación terrestre y aérea.
Oscuro y pequeño
la enfermedad que transmite
      de alta mortalidad en la niñez,
         peligrosa en los ancianos.
Muy posible que ocurra un brote en Nicaragua.
      Recursos materiales. Financieros.
Una intensiva campaña de propaganda.
El aporte de todos los organismos: Salud,
Transporte, Educación, Fuerza Aérea . . .
      La participación de los trabajadores, estudiantes . . .
Y miro las caras serias en torno de la gran mesa
      donde hay cartapacios, ceniceros,
y pienso: qué curioso,
qué curioso. Es el amor:
      El gabinete reunido por el amor al prójimo.

Cabinet Meeting

Scheduled for a cabinet meeting,
knowing beforehand that the issue's very important
but not knowing what it is.
All the ministers and directors of autonomous entities
      at the big table.
And it was a serious matter:
The formation of a National Emergency Committee
to meet the danger from a plague of *Aedes aegypti* mosquitoes.
They especially breed in artificial receptacles.
      You can tell them by their plated lines on the thorax.
It's the female that stings human beings.
She needs blood for her eggs
which she deposits in any receptacle that holds water.
We have to launch a preventative campaign in
flower pots, jars, old tires, barrels, gutters,
      the elimination of useless objects,
          cleanliness in the yards,
              ground and air fumigations.
Dark and small
the illness it transmits
      a high mortality rate among children,
         dangerous to the old.
An outbreak very possible in Nicaragua.
      Material resources. Financial ones.
An intensive public education campaign.
Contributions from all departments: Health,
Transportation, Education, the Air Force . . .
      The participation of workers, students . . .
And I look at the serious faces around the big table
      where there are notebooks, ashtrays,
and I think: how curious,
how curious. It is love:
      The cabinet assembled for love of one's neighbor.

Waslala

Ahora todo es alegre en Waslala.
      Waslala, lindo nombre.
(Antes el sólo nombre aterrorizaba).
Ya no vienen más los campesinos vendados y amarrados.
El atardecer ya no trae gemidos desgarradores
sin sones de guitarra.
Sin aquellos seres que gritaban:
          "Viva la guardia, abajo el pueblo".
Han venido muchachas del Cuá muy contentas, con flores en la cabeza.
Ya pasó la pesadilla: "Waslala".
      Está alegre Waslala, la
capital del terror y la muerte para los campesinos del norte.
Era la cabecera del plan integral contrainsurgente,
del cerco estratégico de aniquilamiento guerrillero.
La peor de las "aldeas estratégicas" de represión campesina.
Ya no están con perros pastor-alemán para rastrear revolucionarios.
      Este risueño rincón de la montaña
que fue lo más tenebroso de la noche de Nicaragua.
Mataban a todos en el rancho.
          Quemaban vivos en el rancho.
      Waslala ya sin las bestias.
Estas tierras para el maíz eran mudos cementerios.
      A veces enterradas familias enteras.
Ya Pancho está con el machete desyerbando el maizal.
Para irse a bañar al río no hay que pedir permiso al cuartel.
La escuela de Waslala tendrá maestros y no a los de la Seguridad.
Los soldados verde-olivo juegan con los niños.
      Los campos ya no son de concentración.
Ya no ruge el helicóptero sobre los cerros
con campesinos, volviendo a los minutos con solo tripulación.
      Aquí traían los de Dudú,
          los de Kubalí,
          los de Kuskawás,
          los de Wanawás,
          los de Zinica,

Waslala

Now all is joyous in Waslala.
   Waslala, lovely name.
(Before the very name spelled terror.)
Now the peasants no longer come blindfolded and tied up.
Nightfall no longer brings heart-rending moans
but the sounds of guitars.
Without those creatures who shouted:
     "Long live the guard, down with the people."
The girls from Cuá have come, so happy, with flowers in their hair.
Now the nightmare "Waslala" is over.
    Waslala is joyous, the
capital of terror and death for the peasants of the north.
The key seat of the entire counterinsurgency plan,
the strategic site for guerrilla annihilation.
The worst "strategic hamlet" of peasant repression.
Now they're no longer there with German shepherds to track down
            revolutionaries.
    This pleasant corner in the mountains
that was the darkest of Nicaragua's night.
They killed everyone at the hut.
      They burned them alive at the hut.
   Waslala now without the beasts.
These lands meant for growing corn were silent cemeteries.
    Sometimes whole families buried.
Now Pancho is there with his machete weeding the cornfield.
You don't have to ask permission at the garrison to bathe in the river.
The Waslala school will have teachers and not members of the Security
            Forces.
The soldiers dressed in olive-green play with the children.
    The fields are no longer concentration camps.
The helicopter no longer roars over the hills
carrying peasants, later returning with just the crew.
    Here they brought people from Dudú,
        from Kubalí,
        from Kuskawás,
        from Wanawás,
        from Zinica,

                    los del Zapote.
Aquí fueron calabozos, fueron cárceles subterráneas,
fueron los fosos con hombres, mujeres, niños y ancianos.
El monte está ya sin las fieras con uniforme de camuflaje.
Los campesinos que vienen de otro lado duermen en el cuartel.
                    Cinco años fue la noche.
Qué bella está esta mañana la montaña,
la montaña donde anduvieron entre los monos tantos guerrilleros.
Frente al comando los niños corren como colibríes.
Frente al CDS las mujeres charlan entre flores como tucanes.
Las banderas roji-negras parecen pájaros.
Qué bello el verde de los campos y el verde de los compas.
Qué lindo resbala ahora el río Waslala.
                    De pronto vino el día.
El café será bueno este año.
Qué alegre está Waslala.

from Zapote.
Here were the lockups, the underground jails,
there were pits holding men, women, children, and the elderly.
The hills are now without the beasts in camouflage uniforms.
The peasants coming from the other side of the mountain sleep in the
garrison.
The night lasted five years.
How beautiful the mountain is this morning,
the mountain where so many guerrilla fighters roamed among the monkeys.
In front of the outpost the children run like hummingbirds.
In front of the CDS the women talk among the flowers like toucans.
The red-and-black flags look like birds.
How beautiful the green of the field and the green of the soldiers.
How lovely the Waslala River flows now.
All at once the day came.
The coffee crop will be good this year.
How joyous Waslala is.

Ecología

En septiembre por San Ubaldo se vieron más coyotes.
Más cuajipales, a poco del triunfo,
  en los ríos, allá por San Ubaldo.
          En la carretera más conejos, culumucos . . .
La población de pájaros se ha triplicado, nos dicen,
  en especial la de los piches.
Los bulliciosos piches bajan a nadar adonde ven el agua brillar.
Los somocistas también destruían los lagos, ríos, y montañas.
  Desviaban el curso de los ríos para sus fincas.
El Ochomogo se había secado el verano pasado.
El Sinecapa secado por el despale de los latifundistas.
El Río Grande de Matagalpa, secado, durante la guerra,
          allá por los llanos de Sébaco.
Dos represas pusieron al Ochomogo,
              y los desechos químicos capitalistas
caían en el Ochomogo y los pescados andaban como borrachos.
      El río de Boaco con aguas negras.
La laguna de Moyuá se había secado. Un coronel somocista
robó las tierras de los campesinos, y construyó una represa.
La laguna de Moyuá que por siglos estuvo bella en ese sitio.
        (Pero ya volverán los pescaditos).
Despalaron y represaron.
            Pocos garrobos al sol, pocos cusucos.
La tortuga verde del Caribe la vendía Somoza.
En camiones exportaban los huevos de paslama y las iguanas.
        Acabándose la tortuga caguama.
El pez-sierra del Gran Lago acabándolo José Somoza.
En peligro de extinción el tigrillo de la selva,
    su suave piel color de selva,
y el puma, el danto en las montañas
          (como los campesinos en las montañas).
¡Y pobre el Río Chiquito! Su desgracia,
la de todo el país. Reflejado en sus aguas el somocismo.
El Río Chiquito de León, alimentado de manantiales
de cloacas, desechos de fábricas de jabón y curtiembres,
agua blanca de fábricas de jabón, roja la de las curtiembres;

Ecology

You saw more coyotes near San Ubaldo in September.
And more alligators, a little after the triumph,
   in the rivers, there near San Ubaldo.
      More rabbits and racoons on the road . . .
The bird population has tripled, they say,
   especially the *piches*.
The noisy *piches* go swim wherever they see the water shining.
The Somocistas destroyed the lakes, rivers, and mountains too.
   They diverted the course of the rivers for their farms.
The Ochomogo had dried up last summer.
The Sinecapa dried up because the landowners stripped the land.
The Rio Grande of Matagalpa dried up during the war,
      there near the Sebaco Plains.
They built two dams on the Ochomogo,
        and the capitalist chemical wastes
spilled into the Ochomogo and the fish reeled around like drunks.
    The Boaco River carried sewage.
The Moyuá Lagoon dried up. A Somocista colonel
robbed the peasants' land and built a dam.
The Moyuá Lagoon that for centuries had been beautiful in that spot.
   (But the little fish will soon return.)
They stripped the land and built dams
      Few *garrobos* in the sun, few armadillos.
Somoza sold the Caribbean green tortoise.
They exported *paslama* and iguana eggs by the truckload.
   The caguama tortoise finished.
The Gran Lago swordfish finished off by José Somoza.
Facing danger of extinction the jungle jaguar,
   its soft skin the color of the jungle,
and the puma, the tapir in the mountains
      (like the peasants in the mountains).
And the poor Chiquito River! Its misfortune
that of the whole country. Somocismo reflected in its waters.
The Chiquito River of León, fed by brooks
of sewage, soap factory and tannery wastes,
white water from the soap factories, red from the tanneries;

plásticos en el lecho, vacinillas, hierros sarrosos. Eso
nos dejó el somocismo.
(Hay que verlo otra vez bonito y claro cantando hacia el mar).
Y al lago de Managua todas las aguas negras de Managua
y los desechos químicos.
                    Y allá por Solentiname, en la isla La Zanata:
un gran cerro blanco y hediondo de esqueletos de pez-sierra.
Pero ya respiraron los pez-sierra y el tiburón de agua dulce.
Tisma está llena otra vez de garzas reales
                              reflejadas en sus espejos.
Tiene muchos zanatillos, piches, güises, zarcetas.
            La flora también se ha beneficiado.
Los cusucos andan muy contentos con este gobierno.
            Recuperaremos los bosques, ríos, lagunas.
Vamos a descontaminar el lago de Managua.
La liberación no soló la ansiaban los humanos.
Toda la ecología gemía. La revolución
es también de lagos, ríos, árboles, animales.

plastics, chamber pots, rusty iron in the riverbed. This
is what Somocismo left us.
(We have to see the river pretty and clear once again singing its way to the
sea).

And into Lake Managua all of Managua's waste waters
and chemical wastes.
            And there near Solentiname, on La Zanata Island:
a great white stinking heap of swordfish skeletons.
But the swordfish and freshwater sharks are breathing again.
Tisma is full of royal herons again
                        reflected in its mirrors.
It has many little starlings, *piches, güises*, widgets.
            The plant life has benefited too.
The armadillos are very happy with this government.
            We will restore our forests, rivers, lagoons.
We will decontaminate Lake Managua.
Not only humans longed for liberation.
All ecology groaned for it also. The revolution
is also one of lakes, rivers, trees, animals.

Las tortugas

Era en el Pacífico.
        Frente a las costas de Nicaragua.
Estábamos pescando pargos rojos
en el mar azul con el cielo azul
        el mar como tinta azul
y de pronto dos tortugas, enganchadas
la una montada sobre la otra
        haciendo el amor en el mar
como lo han venido haciendo desde el principio de su especie
para reproducirse y producir más especies y más especies
el mismo acto en el mar por millones de años
por amor
a la especie humana
y a su culminación
el comunismo.
El acto que se ha venido haciendo desde el principio del mundo.
Y pienso en Mateo 19, 12:
también está el que no se casa
por amor al reino de los cielos, al comunismo
como una tortuga sola en mitad del Pacífico
        sola bajo el cielo
            desposada con el cielo.

The Turtles

It was in the Pacific.
        Facing the Nicaraguan coast.
We were fishing for red snapper
in the blue sea with the blue sky
        the sea like blue ink
and suddenly two turtles, coupled
the one mounted over the other
        making love in the sea
as they had been doing since the beginning of their species
to reproduce themselves and produce more species and more species
the same act in the sea for millions of years
for love
of the human species
and at its culmination
communism.
The act that's been in the making since the beginning of the world.
And I think of Matthew 19,12:
there is also he who does not marry
for love of the kingdom of heaven, of communism
like a lone turtle in the middle of the Pacific
        alone under the sky
           wed to heaven.

Fundación de la Asociación Latinoamericana para los Derechos Humanos

La sala de conferencias en forma de anfiteatro,
                     funcional, de
genuino no-estilo,
         típica arquitectura intercontinental,
              delicadamente forrada
de tosco material cremoso, textura incitante al tacto,
y donde el plywood pardo relumbra bajo la luz dorada
arrojada por cilindros plateados desde el techo blanco de
         plástico y más aún
por los cegadores reflectores, y los flashs de los fotógrafos;
donde la hilera de banderas latinoamericanas
es una sola mezcla de colores patrios sin fronteras
tras el estrado en que está la mesa directiva
con los luminosos vasos de agua efervescente
y el podium con el micrófono niquelado refulgente ante los
         reflectores: la sala esta de Quito,
              la veo hoy, desde mi puesto en el estrado
              curiosamente, llena de animales.
Hay ex-presidentes. Personalidades importantes.
Desde la iguana se llegó lentamente a esta especie
que está sentada en esta sala de conferencias
y desde el micrófono denuncia los regímenes facistas.

Artículo 16: El Comité Ejecutivo tiene las siguientes funciones:

Somos animal, cada uno separado, individuales.
              Animal igual que la iguana.
              Aunque se nos nombre animal racional.
Pero juntos NO somos animal, somos el hombre:
el hombre, por ejemplo, en esta sala, defendiendo al hombre
         sus derechos humanos.
Somos una especie singular, con anteojos, con corbata, con
         peinados.
De la vida en los palos a estas ponencias hay mucho avance.
Somos un extraño ser mirándose, sonriéndose, conversándose
         en esta sala:

Founding of the Latin American
Human Rights Association

The conference hall in the form of an amphitheater,
                                    functional, in
a genuine nonstyle,
            typical international architecture,
                    delicately covered
with a coarse, creamy material, a texture exciting to the touch,
and where the brown plywood shines beneath the golden light
hurled down by silver-plated cylinders from the white ceiling of
        plastic and even more so
by the blinding spotlights, and the flashbulbs of the photographers;
where the row of Latin American flags
is just one mixture of borderless national colors
behind the dais where the board of directors sits
with luminous glasses of sparkling water
and the podium with its nickel-plated microphone radiant in front of the
        spotlights: this hall in Quito,
            I see it today, from my place on the dais,
                    curiously, full of animals.
There are ex-presidents. Important personalities.
From the iguana things slowly arrived at this species
that is seated in this conference hall
and that from the microphone denounces fascist regimes.

Article 16: The Executive Committee has the following functions:

We are animal, each one separate, individual.
                Animal the same as the iguana.
            Even though we are named rational animal.
But together we are NOT animal, we are humanity:
humanity, for example, in this hall, defending humanity's
                human rights.
We are a singular species, with spectacles, with necktie, with
        hair styles.
From life in the trees to these talks there's a great advance,
We are some strange being conversing, smiling, looking at one another
        in this hall:

75

un ser diverso y uno.
En la sala sólo hay Uno
en muchos asientos, levantándose aquel,
sacando un cigarrillo el otro,
                    este otro fotografiando a los demás.
Los arauacos se daban a sí mismos ese nombre,
          arawak: que quiere decir "hombre"
                    "gente".
Dice Ruth Benedict que los Zuñi, los Dané, los Kiowa
se dieron esos nombres, que quieren decir: "seres humanos"
          aunque estaban rodeados de otros pueblos.
Los Koguis colombianos: su nombre es "gente".
                    Mis amigos Yaruros: su nombre es "gente".
          Y en Antioquía, en aquel internado indígena
un joven Páez me dijo que el nombre de ellos no es Páez sino
          Naza
                    "que quiere decir gente o persona".
Los animales se adaptan biológicamente
al medio ambiente, y sus adaptaciones son hereditarias.
                    (De ahí las especies.)
Las adaptaciones del hombre son culturales,
no sujetas a herencia. Por lo que Pablo dijo:
                    "no hay judío ni griego".
Me quedo largamente mirando mi especie
aunque me ofuscan los flashs y los reflectores.
Señores: la solidaridad con Bolivia, con El Salvador
es un esfuerzo humano que arranca desde la hermana iguana.

a being that is diverse and one.
          In this hall there's only One
in many seats, that one standing up,
another one taking out a cigarette,
                    this other one photographing the others.
The Araucans gave themselves the name,
          Arawak: which means "human being"
                    "people."
Ruth Benedict says that the Zunis, the Danes, the Kiowas
gave themselves those names that mean: "human beings"
          even though they were surrounded by other peoples.
The Colombian Koguis: their name is "people."
                    My Yaruro friends: their name is "folk."
          And in Antioquía, in that aboriginal boarding school
a young Páez told me that their name isn't Páez but
     Naza
                    "which means folk or persons."
Animals biologically adapt themselves
to the environment, and their adaptations are hereditary.
                                        (Thus the species.)

Human adaptations are cultural,
not tied to heredity. According to Paul:
                    "there is neither Jew nor Greek."
I remain looking at length at my species
although flashbulbs and spotlights blind me.
Ladies and gentlemen: solidarity with Bolivia, with El Salvador
is a human endeavor that began with our sister and brother the iguana.

Misa ecuménica en Düsseldorf

Cuántos rostros juntos,
      son como 2.000 jóvenes,
miles de pelos rubios, trigal ondulante,
el sol tras los ventanales haciendo rebrillar el trigal,
ondulante bajo el vaivén del viento de la música electrónica.
Les doy la comunión, con
      cestas de pan rubio, y vino rubio del Rhin
en vasitos de cartón. Tantos
      trigos juntos en un sólo pan
      tantas uvas doradas en un sólo vino.
Y también todos unidos en el canto.
      Tanto canto unido,
tantas gargantas juntas en la palabra del canto.
Y todos sonrientes, tantas sonrisas juntas
como un solo rostro sonriente.
Un rostro de 2.000 rostros
      iluminado por el sol de los ventanales,
algo de la gloria de los cuerpos resucitados, pienso yo.
Por el rostro somos humanos. Los animales
son sin rostro.
      (Y no distinguen nuestros rostros.
El perro diferencia millones de olores, no los rostros,
pero nosotros distinguimos infinitud de rostros).
¿Es esto lo de
      "a su imagen y semejanza"?
Este es el ser social que Dios creó en el principio, pienso yo,
      social y uno,
      "varón y mujer *lo* creó".
Todos los rostros formaban juntos un sólo rostro de todos
      y un sólo rostro de uno.
En la superficie del planeta
Düsseldorf cada vez más cerca de Solentiname.
Y la unión en las peticiones.
Uno: "Señor,
      que en Nicaragua se realice todo lo que allí sueñan".
Y otro oró:
      "Que en el mundo haya muchas Nicaraguas".

Ecumenical Mass in Düsseldorf

How many faces together,
        there are some 2,000 youths,
thousands of blonds, a waving wheatfield,
the sun behind the church windows making the wheatfield shine,
waving under the swaying winds of electronic music.
I offer them communion, with
        baskets of white bread, and golden yellow Rhine wine
in cardboard cups. So many
        grains of wheat together in one single loaf
        so many golden grapes in one single wine.
And also all united in song.
        So much united song,
so many throats together in the words of the song.
And all smiling, so many smiles together
like a single smiling face.
A face made out of 2,000 faces
        lit up by the sun through the church windows,
something of the glory of reborn bodies, I think.
Our faces make us human. Animals
are faceless.
        (And they can't distinguish our faces.
Dogs can discern millions of odors, but not faces,
while we distinguish an infinity of faces.)
Is this what's meant by
        "in God's image and likeness"?
This is the social being God created in the beginning, I think,
        social and one,
        "male and female God created them one."
All the faces together formed one single face for all
        and one single face for one.
On the surface of the planet
Düsseldorf ever closer to Solentiname.
And the union in their prayers.
One: "Lord,
        let all that is dreamed in Nicaragua be realized."
And another prayed:
        "Let there be many Nicaraguas in the world."

Concentración en St. George

Mar azul, más azul en partes,
    verdoso (en manchas) y más verde.
Ciertas rocas grandes con olas reventando
    —blanco sobre el azul.
El cielo azul es pálido ante el azulísimo mar.
Triangulitos blancos en el azul.
    Iglesia blanca contra el azul del mar.
      Una isla de tarjeta postal.
Las casas inglesas y francesas se distinguen por sus techos.
Esta isla cambiaba de manos como bola de tenis.
    Cocos y palmeras.
      Los almendros de ramas horizontales.
Chilamates, sus raíces colgando de ramas buscando la tierra.
Ves la nuez moscada y la canela entre las lianas.
    Casas pobres entre bugambilias.
La humanidad aquí es de color de tierra.
Tierra café, y tierra negra mojada
      humus húmedo.
Helechos, plátanos, hojas gruesas, hojas de colores.
Hojas de Henri Rousseau bordeando la estrecha carretera.
Cactus carnosos. Vimos desde un puente
    mujeres lavando ropa con los pechos desnudos.
Rótulos revolucionarios entre los flamboyanes y frutas-de-pan.
    El dulce perfume de los frangipani.
Plantas que el jardinero de mi abuela cuidaba
      aquí son silvestres.
No hay culebras venenosas en esta isla.
Todos los tonos de verdes resaltando sobre verdes.
Una muchacha morada, en su palma anaranjada una almendra roja.
Las casitas blancas entre lo verde.
Los barcos muy blancos sobre el azul.
En inglés se pronuncia *Greneida*.
Negrita en pantaloncitos cortos como fruta tropical.
La piel de sus piernas parece sonreírnos.
    —Toda su piel como negros labios sonrientes.
Esta isla la conoció Colón.

Mass Rally in St. George

Blue sea, some parts bluer,
    greenish (in patches) and greener still.
Some great rocks with breaking waves
    —white on blue.
The blue sky is pale against the deep blue sea.
Small white triangles in the blue.
    White church against the blue of the sea.
    A picture postcard island.
You can tell the English from the French houses by their rooftops.
This island changed hands like a tennis ball.
    Coconuts and palm trees.
    Almond trees with horizontal branches.
Chilamates, with their roots hanging from branches that seek the earth.
Look at the nutmeg nuts and cinnamon among the vines.
    Humble shacks among the bougainvilleas.
Here humanity is earthcolored.
Brown earth, and damp black earth
    humid humus.
Ferns, plantains, thick leaves, colored leaves.
Henri Rousseau leaves fringing the narrow road.
Fat cacti. From a bridge we saw
    women washing clothes, their breasts bare.
Revolutionary signs among the poincianas and breadfruits.
    The sweet perfume of the jasmines.
Plants my grandmother's gardener tended
    grow wild here.
There are no venemous snakes on this island.
All the tones of green, greens projecting out over greens.
A purple girl, a red almond in her orange hand.
The small, white houses amidst the green.
The boats very white on the blue.
In English it's pronounced Grenayda.
Black girl in little short pants, like tropical fruit.
The skin of her legs seems to smile at us.
    —All her skin like smiling black lips.
Columbus knew this island.

Junto al mar es la gran concentración.
Verde de la vegetación y verde-olivo de los uniformes.
Ves
la belleza de la naturaleza y la belleza de la Revolución.
El eco de la ovación a Bishop
por toda la bahía de St. George.
Ves arenas doradas aquí, plateadas más allá y mar turquesa.
Una negra comiendo un mango amarillo en la concentración.
Aplauden moviendo el cuerpo, danzando.
Filas de banderines de papel aleteando en el cielo, al fondo
un trozo de mar azul rosa.
Adolescente negra con sweater rojo y pechos grandes como cocos.
Concentración de abigarrados colores como flores y frutas.
Una isla de 120 millas cuadradas y 110 mil habitantes
(sus 350 milicianos con uniformes que regaló Nicaragua)
una islita sola en el océano desafiando al imperialismo.

The mass meeting is by the sea.
Green of the vegetation and olive-green of the uniforms.
You see
the beauty of nature and the beauty of Revolution.
The echoing ovation for Bishop
from all over St. George harbor.
You see golden sands here, silver ones further on and the turquoise sea.
A black woman eating a yellow mango at the mass meeting.
They applaud moving their bodies, dancing.
Rows of paper flags fluttering in the sky, in the background
a bit of pink-blue sea.
An adolescent black girl with a red sweater and large breasts like coconuts.
A mass meeting of motley colors like flowers and fruits.
An island of 120 square miles and 110 thousand inhabitants
(their 350 militia soldiers with uniforms Nicaragua gave them)
a tiny island alone in the ocean defying imperialism.

Las loras

Mi amigo Michel es responsable militar en Somoto,
       allá por la frontera con Honduras,
y me contó que descubrió un contrabando de loras
que iban a ser exportadas a EE. UU.
       para que allí aprendieran a hablar inglés.
Eran 186 loras, y ya habían muerto 47 en sus jaulas.
Y él las regresó al lugar de donde las habían traído,
y cuando el camión estaba llegando a un lugar
          que llaman Los Llanos
cerea de las montañas de donde eran esas loras
      (las montañas se veían grandes
          detrás de esos llanos)
las loras comenzaron a agitarse y a batir sus alas
      y a apretujarse contra las paredes de sus jaulas.
Y cuando les abrieron las jaulas
todas volaron como flechas en la misma dirección
          a sus montañas.
Eso mismo hizo la Revolución con nosotros, pienso yo:
nos sacó de las jaulas
      en las que nos llevaban a hablar inglés.
Nos devolvió la patria de la que nos habían arrancado.

Los compas verdes como loras
      dieron a las loras sus montañas verdes.
     Pero hubo 47 que murieron.

The Parrots

My friend Michel is the military leader in Somoto,
          there near the border with Honduras,
and he told me he discovered a contraband shipment of parrots
set for export to the U.S.
          so that there they would learn to speak English.
There were 186 parrots, and 47 had already died in their cages.
And he sent them back where they'd come from,
and when the truck reached a place
                    they call The Plains
near the mountain homes of these parrots
          (the mountains looked huge
                              rising from these plains)
the parrots began to stir and beat their wings
          and jam themselves against their cage walls.
And when the cages were opened
they all flew out like arrows in the same direction
                              toward their mountains.
This is the same thing, I think, that the Revolution did to us:
it took us out of the cages
                    in which they'd carried us off to speak English.
It brought us back the homeland from which they'd uprooted us.

The soldiers green like parrots
                    gave the parrots their green mountains.
          But there were 47 who died.

Visión mística de las letras FSLN

Sobre el cerro Motastepe, en las cercanías de Managua
un gran anuncio en letras blancas
ROLTER
se veía desde muchas calles de Managua
y el niño Juan me preguntó yendo en un automóvil
qué querían decir esas letrotas
ROLTER
y le dije que una marca de zapatos
y era para que la gente comprara los zapatos.
"¿Pero cuando triunfe la Revolución ya no habrá esos anuncios
verdad?" me dijo el niño.
Fue pocos días antes de la ofensiva de octubre
lo que él no sabía
días angustiosos para mí.
Esa tarde él jugó con otros niños a sandinistas y guardias
pero el problema era, dijeron, que nadie quería ser guardia.
Muchas veces después del triunfo, las grandes letras
me recordaban las palabras de Juan, aún sin cumplirse.
Desde hace un año vemos desde muchas calles de Managua
en el cerro en vez de esas letras otras:
FSLN
y yo muchas veces también recordando lo del niño con alegría.
Era un domingo a mediodía con el cielo sombrío.
Y hay días en que uno pide una señal.
Soledades muy íntimas. Como
cuando Santa Teresita en su lecho de agonía
sentía la duda de si Dios existe.
Entonces desde el auto miré las letras grandes sobre el cerro
y dentro de mí me habló Dios:
"Mirá lo que yo hice por vos,
por tu pueblo, pues.
Mirá esas letras, y no dudés de mí, tené fe
hombre de poca fe
pendejo".

Mystical Vision of the Letters FSLN

On top of Motastepe Hill, on the outskirts of Managua
a large advertisement in white letters
>   ROLTER

could be seen from many streets in Managua
and the little boy Juan riding in an automobile asked me
what those big letters meant
>   ROLTER

and I told him a brand of shoes
and it was so people would buy those shoes.
"But when the Revolution triumphs there won't be those advertisements
right?" the child said to me.
It was a few days before the October Offensive
which he didn't know about
>   anxious days for me.

That afternoon he played Sandinistas and guardsmen with other children
but the problem was, they said, nobody wanted to be a guardsman.
Many times after the triumph the large letters
made me remember Juan's words, even though they didn't come true.
For a year now from many Managua streets
instead of those letters on the hill we see others:
>   FSLN

and I many times also recall the child's words with joy.
>   It was a Sunday at noon with an overcast sky.
>   And there are days when one asks for a sign.

Very intimate solitudes. Like
when Theresa of Lisieux upon her deathbed
would feel doubts about whether God existed.
Then from the car I looked at the large letters on the hill
and from within God spoke to me:
"Behold what I did for you,
>   for your people that is.

Behold those letters, and never doubt me, have faith
man of so little faith
you jerk."

En Managua a media noche

Acostado en mi cama en Managua
iba a dormirme
          y de pronto me pregunto:
          ¿Para dónde vamos? Estamos
en la mitad oscura de la tierra,
               la otra mitad, iluminada.
Mañana estaremos en la luz
y los otros en lo oscuro.
Esta noche acostado en mi cama
siento el viaje. ¿Pero para dónde vamos?
Recuerdo números aprendidos en otro tiempo:
Alrededor del sol a 30 kilómetros por segundo,
y junto con el sol en la galaxia a 250 kilómetros por segundo
¿y la galaxia va a que velocidad . . . ?
Estate tranquilo Felipe Peña caído no sabemos dónde,
y Donald y Elvis enterrados por la frontera con Costa Rica
estén tranquilos muchachos, que vamos bien.
          Girando en el espacio negro
dondequiera que vayamos, vamos bien.
Y también
     va bien la Revolución.

In Managua at Midnight

Lying in my bed in Managua
I was going to sleep
        and suddenly I asked myself:
    Where are we going? We are
on the dark half of the earth,
        the other half, illuminated.
Tomorrow we'll be in the light
and the others in the dark.
Tonight lying in my bed
I feel the trip. But where are we going?
I remember numbers learned in other days:
Around the sun at 30 kilometers per second,
and together with the sun the galaxy at 250 kilometers per second
and the galaxy moves at what velocity? . . .
Rest in peace Felipe Peña fallen we don't know where,
and Donald and Elvis buried on the border with Costa Rica
rest in peace, boys, we're doing fine.
        Turning in the black space
wherever we go, we're doing fine.
And too
    the Revolution is doing fine.

IV

VUELOS DE MEMORIA Y VISIÓN
FLIGHTS OF MEMORY AND VISION

Preguntas frente al lago

Cuando después de dos años volviste, Juan, a Solentiname,
          siendo ya un niño de cinco,
recuerdo muy bien lo que me dijiste:
"¿Vos sos el que me vas a decir todo lo de Dios, verdad?"
Y yo que cada vez
               he ido sabiendo menos de Dios.
Un místico, o sea un amador de Dios
          le llamó NADA,
y otro dijo: todo lo que digas de él es falso.
Y lo mejor para que tuvieras vos conocimiento de Dios
era tal vez que yo no estuviera hablándote de Dios.
Pero una vez
      sí te hablé de Dios, frente al lago,
                              en el muelle,
          un atardecer todo rosa y rosicler:
"Dios es uno que está dentro de todos,
dentro de vos, de mí, en todas partes".
"¿Y está en aquella garza?" "Sí está". "¿Y está en las sardinas?"
"Sí está". "¿Y está en esas nubes?" "Sí está".
"¿Y está en aquella otra garza?" "Sí está".
Un adán chiquito nombrando todo tu pequeño paraíso.
"¿Y está en este muelle?" "Sí está". "¿Y está en las olas?"
¿Por qué los niños preguntan tanto?
¿Y yo
     por qué pregunto por qué
                    como un niño?
"¿Y también está en mi papá y mi mamá?" "Sí está".
Y me dijiste:
          "¿Pero no llega a la isla de los malos, verdad?"
Ahora de 12 años
sos de la Asociación de Niños Sandinistas.
Vas a las concentraciones. Participás en trabajos voluntarios.
Hacés vigilancia revolucionaria. Estás en las milicias.
              (Ya se fueron los de la isla de los malos).
"¿Y está también en las estrellitas
las estrellitas chiquitas que son tan grandes, verdad?"

Questions by the Lake

When, after two years you returned to Solentiname,
                    already a child of five, Juan,
I remember very well what you said to me:
"You're the one who's going to tell me all about God, right?"
And I who all the time
                    have come to know less about God.
A mystic, that is, a lover of God
          called God NOTHING,
and another said: all that you say about God is false.
And if you were to have knowledge of God it was better
perhaps I didn't talk to you of God.
But once
          I certainly spoke to you of God by the lake,
                              on the dock,
          during a twilight all pink and silver:
"God is one who's within all of us,
within you, within me, within everywhere."
"And God is within that heron?" "Yes." "And within the sardines?"
"Yes." "And within those clouds?" "Yes."
"And within that other heron?" "Yes."
A tiny Adam naming all your small paradise.
"And God is within this dock?" "Yes." "And within the waves?"
Why do children ask so many questions?
And I
          why do I question why
                    like a child?
"And God is also within my dad and my mom?" "Yes God is."
And you told me:
          "But God doesn't get to the island of the bad ones, right?"
Now, 12 years old,
you're in the Association of Sandinista Children.
You go to the rallies. You take part in voluntary work.
You take watch turns for the revolution. You're in the militia.
          (Now the bad ones have left their island.)
"And God is also within the little stars
the tiny little stars that are so big, right?"

Los números de lo pequeño
          son tan grandes como los de lo grande.
¿De dónde veniste vos?
Y yo me asombré, no sólo por tus preguntas
sino porque además pensé que
de trecientos millones de espermatozoides
                    sólo fuiste vos, Juan,
de trecientos millones de Juan
distintos del Juan que vos sos
pero gemelos de vos
sólo fuiste vos, una vez.
Y como vos
trecientos millones me preguntaban desde su no existencia
              dónde está Dios,
diciéndome que les diga todo lo de Dios,
            ¿si también está dentro de ellos?
(Y con ellos toda la infinitud de no existentes
infinitamente mayor que lo existente).
Como si me interrogaran de repente
trecientos millones de astros pero no existentes.
Aunque entre todos esos millones,
              en los que también está Dios,
sólo fuiste vos, Juan,
el que me preguntaba aquella tarde en el lago.
          El que creyó un día que yo le diría todo lo de Dios.

The numbers measuring littleness
           are as large as those for bigness.
Where did you come from?
And I was shocked, not only by your questions
but also because I thought that
of three hundred million spermatazoids
                   it was only you, Juan,
of the three hundred million Juans
distinct from the Juan that you are
but twins of you
it was only you, once.
And like you
three hundred million asked me from their nonexistence
           where is God,
telling me I should tell them all about God,
           and if God is also within them?
(And with them the whole infinity of nonexistents
infinitely greater than the existent.)
As if all at once I were interrogated
by three hundred million stars that didn't exist.
Although among all those millions,
           within which God also is,
you were the only one, Juan,
the one who questioned me that day by the lake.
           The one who one day believed that I would tell him all about God.

El cuento de los garrobos

A la Asociación de Niños Sandinistas

Estuve en Niquinohomo y allí me contaron
                    el cuento de un chavalo
que un día de agosto salió a cazar garrobos;
cogió de la estación para allasito,
                    siguiendo la línea del tren;
    allí se encontró con un amigo;
era mediodía y hacía mucho sol,
y habían unos garrobos gordos tomando sol en los palos.
        El chavalo con su pistola se apió el primer garrobo.
Y de pronto vino pitando el tren de "Los Pueblos"
        y se espantaron los otros garrobos.
El tren venía cargado de gente, todos de kaki,
                    parecía que eran soldados nicaragüenses,
pero cuando pasaron el chavalo vió
                que eran marinos yankis
                            que iban para Jinotepe,
y el chavalo se puso furioso
            y dijo que deseaba colgarlos a todos de los palos.
Lo interesante de este cuento es que este chavalo
            después pudo realizar lo que deseaba.
Ahora en Niquinohomo me contaron esta historia
cuando estábamos haciendo museo
                la casa en que vivió ese chavalo.

The Tale of the *Garrobos*

To the Association of Sandinista Children

I was in Niquinohomo and there they told me
                the tale of a boy
who one August day went out to hunt *garrobos;*
he went past the station over yonder,
                   following the train tracks
      to where he met a friend;
it was midday and the sun burned bright,
and some fat *garrobos* were in the trees sunning themselves.
      The boy brought down the first *garrobo* with his pistol.
And suddenly the train of "Los Pueblos" came tooting along
      and startled the other *garrobos.*
The train came filled with people, all in khaki,
          it seemed they were Nicaraguan soldiers,
but when they went by the boy saw
         they were yankee Marines
             on their way to Jinotepe,
and the boy became furious
       and said he wanted to hang them all from the trees.
What's interesting in this tale is that this boy
        later did what he wanted to do.
Just now in Niquinohomo they told me this story
when we were making a museum
       of the house where this boy lived.

Note: The boy in this poem is Sandino; *garrobos* are iguanalike animals native to Nicaragua.

El chancho que no comió Rigoberto

Me contaron esto hace tiempo, me lo contó uno
al que se lo contó otro al que se lo contó otro
          que fué testigo:
y es que Rigoberto López Pérez llegó al Parque Central de León
el 21 de septiembre de 1956, en la tardecita,
              y allí vió unos amigos,
y compró un chancho frito
y se puso a comer el chancho con yuca en una hoja de plátano,
pero casi no comió nada, sólo unos dos bocados,
no tenía hambre,
y tiró el chancho con yuca al suelo con la hoja,
y vió a un obrero muy borracho, y a un mendigo,
y dijo: "Esto se va a acabar ya".
              Y se fue para donde tenía que ir.

The Pork Rigoberto Didn't Eat

They told me this some time ago, I was told by one
that another had told that another who was
        a witness had told:
and it's that Rigoberto López Pérez arrived at the Central Park of León
September 21, 1956, in the evening,
        and there he saw some friends,
and bought some fried pork
and set about eating the pork with yucca in a banana leaf,
but he barely ate anything, only some two mouthfuls,
he wasn't hungry,
and he threw the pork with yucca to the ground with the leaf,
and saw a worker who was very drunk and a beggar,
and he said: "This is going to come to an end now."
        And he went where he had to go.

Note: Rigoberto López Pérez killed Anastasio Somoza García on 21 September 1956.

Recordando de pronto

En mis últimos días en el mundo
cuando yo ya iba a ser un monje trapense
conocí en un balneario una linda muchacha
que iba a ser monja.
                    Era además prima mía.
Recuerdo aquellas piernas.
            Sus curvas como la curva de la costa.
Su piel era morena como la arena de la playa.
Desnuda, excepto lo que cubría el traje de baño.
            Iba a desposarse con Dios.
                ¡Las Bodas con Dios!
Y yo pensé en el buen gusto de Dios.

Madre Ana aún es monja
pero en plena revolución nicaragüense
es monja reaccionaria.

Recalling All of a Sudden

In my last days out in the world
when I was set on becoming a Trappist monk
I met at a beach a lovely girl
who was going to be a nun.
           She was I should add a cousin of mine.
I remember her legs.
        Her curves like the curve of the coast.
Her skin was dark like the sand of the beach.
Nude, except for what her bathing suit covered.
         She was going to marry God.
         A Wedding with God!
And I thought of God's good taste.

Mother Ana is still a nun
but in the full bloom of the Nicaraguan Revolution
she's a reactionary nun.

A Donald y Elvis

Muchachos,
esta es una interesante pregunta:
      ¿Y ustedes por qué son sagrados?
Cómo veríamos ahora el balde con que vos Donald
ordeñabas todas las mañanas.
      Podías ordeñar
      y además escribir un poema sobre tu ordeño:
         El ternero coloca su fea trompa
         acariciando desesperadamente los pezones . . .
Por cierto que—coincidencia—allí donde ordeñabas
se construye la "Escuela Donald Guevara"
para formación de líderes campesinos.
Y tu guitarra Elvis está en la "Biblioteca Elvis Chavarría"
en Managua, frente a un mercado,
               donde leen los niños del mercado
(recuerdo esa característica tuya, tu ternura por los niños
y principalmente por ellos entraste al Frente,
         la desnutrición, la mortalidad infantil,
y moriste por ellos principalmente).
Ahora hay dos barcos blancos que cruzan el lago,
el barco "Donald Guevara" y el barco "Elvis Chavarría".
Como también hay ahora en Solentiname
      la isla Donald Guevara y la isla Elvis Chavarría.
Guardamos para un museo las cuerdas de nylon verde,
      verlas me dió escalofrío,
con que ataron sus manos a la espalda, y así fueron enterrados
asesinados por la guardia en una hacienda de Somoza
      junto al Río Frío.
Se distinguen las cuerdas del uno y las del otro
porque un lazo es más estrecho y otro más ancho
y Elvis tenía unas manotas más anchas.
Cuando ví los huesos desenterrados de los dos
te recordé Donald diciendo en la misa de Solentiname
que la resurrección no eran las quirinas saliendo de las tumbas
sino la supervivencia de la conciencia en los otros.
Ustedes habían leído antes un folletito del Frente

To Donald and Elvis

Boys,
here's an interesting question:
        And why is it that you are so sacred?
How would we now see the bucket you used then, Donald,
to milk the cows in the mornings?
        You could milk the cows
        and also write a poem about your milking:
            The calf positions his ugly snout
            desperately caressing her teats . . .
Surely it's a coincidence that they're building
the "Donald Guevara School" for training peasant leaders
there where you milked the cows.
And your guitar, Elvis, is in the "Elvis Chavarría Library"
in Managua, in front of a market,
                where market children read
(I recall that trait of yours, your tenderness toward children,
and mainly because of them you entered the Front,
            the malnutrition, the infant mortality,
and you died mainly for them).
Today there are two white boats that cross the lake,
the "Donald Guevara" boat and the "Elvis Chavarría" boat.
Just as in Solentiname there are now
        a Donald Guevara Island and an Elvis Chavarría Island.
We're saving the green nylon strings for a museum,
        seeing them gives me the chills,
strings used to tie your hands behind your backs, that's how you were buried,
murdered by the guards in a hacienda that belonged to Somoza
        next to the Frío River.
We can tell one set of strings from the other
because one is narrower and the other wider
and Elvis had the wider hands.
When I saw the disinterred bones of the two of you
I remembered you Donald in the Solentiname Mass saying
that the Resurrection was not skeletons coming out of the tombs
but survival in the consciousness of others.
Before, both of you had read a Frente pamphlet

para aspirantes a militantes
donde se decía todo lo que podía pasarle al militante:
encarcelado, encapuchado, golpeado, castrado, sacados los ojos,
             enterrado vivo, quemado vivo.
Pero que no hablaran.
             Y torturaban más mientras más se hablaba.
Quisiéramos tener Donald tu bote que tanto querías
no para que navegue sino para que nadie lo toque.
Recuerdo Elvis la noche que llegaste borracho sin que lo notáramos
y subiste a acostarte al tabanco del rancho
y caía un líquido sobre la mesa donde yo escribía mi poesía:
ahora para nosotros esa vomitada se volvió sagrada.
Santa Teresita de Lisieux a los trece años
             (entonces no se llamaba así)
en Roma besó la arena del Coliseo.
—Aunque parece que no morían en el Coliseo sino en el Circo Máximo.
Hay conventos de monjitas, que como de algo tienen que vivir,
             viven de la venta de reliquias
un hilo de la sotana de San Juan Bosco,
un polvito de huesito de San Caralampio.
Así también la Revolución tiene sus reliquias y mártires.
La voz campesina de Felipe guardada en un cassette
             también es sagrada.
                    La otra de las tres islas grandes es la Felipe Peña.
Donald, Elvis, y Felipe que murió sin tumba,
             ustedes ahora son santos
como aquel santo que salió del seminario
y dijo que todos debíamos vivir como los santos.
Que ningún dogmático aunque sea el Arzobispo de Managua
venga a negarnos que ustedes están vivos (aunque él no lo cree)
             y que además son sagrados.
Dios quiera que yo algún día fuera sagrado como ustedes.
Para la eternidad todo lo de ustedes ha quedado grabado
hasta cualquiera de sus gritos jugando fútbol.
             El lago de Nicaragua reflejando el cielo
                    es todo de ustedes.
             El cielo que en el agua se refleja
                    es de ustedes.
Mientras el "Elvis Chavarría" viene y el "Donald Guevara" va.

written for those wanting to become militants
and stating all that could happen to one who joined:
imprisoned, hooded, beaten, castrated, eyes pulled out,
            buried alive, burned alive.
But they didn't talk.
            And to the degree they did, they were tortured more.
Donald, we would like to have the boat you loved so much
not to sail it but to see that no one would ever touch it.
I remember, Elvis, the night you came in drunk without our noticing it
and you climbed up and lay down in the stalls of the cabin
and a liquid fell over the table where I was writing my poetry:
now for us that vomit's become sacred.
Saint Theresa of Lisieux at age 13
            (that wasn't her name then)
kissed the Coliseum sand in Rome.
—Although it seems they didn't die in the Coliseum, but rather in the
                                          Maximus Circus.
There are convents of nuns who, since they must live from something,
            live by selling relics
a thread from Saint John Bosco's robe,
a bit of dust from a bit of San Caralampio's bones.
So the Revolution also has its relics and martyrs.
The peasant voice of Felipe saved on a cassette
            is also sacred.
                  The other of the three large islands is Felipe Peña Island.
Donald, Elvis, and Felipe who died without tomb,
            now you are saints
like that saint who came out of the seminary
and said we should all live as the saints do.
So that no dogmatist even if it's the Archbishop of Managua
can come to us denying you two are alive (even though he doesn't believe it)
            and that you are also sacred.
May God grant that one day I may be as sacred as you.
For eternity all about you has been recorded
even all your shouts as you played soccer.
            Lake Nicaragua reflecting the sky
                  is completely yours.
            The sky reflected in the water
                  is yours.
While the "Elvis Chavarría" comes and the "Donald Guevara" goes.

Elvis

Elvis Chavarría, soñé que estabas vivo en tu isla Fernando
de Solentiname, la isla de tu mamá
como si no hubieras caído
          después de tu asalto al cuartel de San Carlos,
y me ibas a llevar a conocer un nuevo hijo tuyo,
          como la niña que antes habías tenido,
la chavalita morenita
          que se te atribuía a vos y era igualita a vos
y yo te envidiaba por este nuevo hijo,
porque podías hacer lo que me está negado, porque me lo he negado yo,
y entonces desperté y recordé que estabas muerto
y que tu isla Fernando ahora se llama isla Elvis Chavarría,
y ya no podías tener ese nuevo hijito que se parecía a vos
como tampoco yo,
          estabas muerto igual que yo
aunque estamos vivos los dos.

Elvis

Elvis Chavarría, I dreamt you were alive on your Fernando Island
in Solentiname, the island of your mama,
as if you had not fallen
      when you attacked the San Carlos garrison,
and you were going to take me to see a new child of yours,
      like the girl you'd had before,
the dark, little girl
      that was said to be yours and looked just like you
and I envied you for having this new child,
because you could do what's denied to me, because I have denied it to myself,
and then I awoke and remembered you were dead
and that Fernando Island is now called Elvis Chavarría Island
and now you couldn't have this new little child who looked like you
just as I couldn't,
      you were dead just like me
although we're both very much alive.

A Ernesto Castillo mi sobrino

Recuerdo Ernesto cuando volviste de tu entrenamiento
y hablabas de armas "lindísimas" que habías aprendido a manejar,
   ". . . es linda, mamá" le decías a tu mamá,
como quien habla de la belleza de una muchacha.
Después una bala de francotirador te dio en la cara
cuando saltabas a la calle en León
gritando para animar a los de tu escuadra que te seguían:
                    ¡PATRIA LIBRE O MORIR!
Poeta caído a los 20 años.
Estoy pensando en esto Ernesto
ahora que los niños son besados por los soldados
y hay un taller de poesía en la Policía
y el ejército de Alfabetización con su uniforme azul y gris
está regado por todo el país, y hay Reforma Agraria
y los niños vendeperiódicos y limpiabotas son llevados a jugar
y . . . bueno, de verdad que fueron lindísimas esas armas
   (y recuerdo el brillo de tus ojos cuando lo decías).

To Ernesto Castillo My Nephew

I remember, Ernesto, when you returned from your training
and spoke about the "lovely" weapons you'd learned to handle,
     ". . . it's lovely, mom," you would tell your mother,
like someone talking about a girl's beauty.
Later a sniper's bullet got you in the face
when you leaped into the streets of León
shouting to encourage those from your squadron following you:
     FREE HOMELAND OR DEATH!
A poet fallen at the age of 20.
I'm thinking about this, Ernesto,
now that children receive kisses from the soldiers
and the Police have a poetry workshop
and the army of Literacy Teachers with their blue and gray uniforms
is sent throughout the country, and there's an Agrarian Reform
and the newspaper and shoeshine boys are taken out to play
and . . . well, those weapons really were lovely
     (and I remember the sparkle in your eyes when you'd say it).

Viaje muy jodido

Aquella telefoneada inesperada de Managua
        a la última isla de las Antillas:
    "Ernesto, murió Laureano".
En el vuelo Trinidad-Barbados-Jamaica-Habana-Managua
        mirando mar, y mar, no podía pensar en otra cosa.
Ya que hemos nacido desahuciados
lo mejor es morir Héroe y Mártir
      como vos moriste.
Claro que hubiera sido mejor que no murieras nunca,
con tal que tu esposa y tus hijos y tus amigos y el mundo entero
no murieran nunca.
Cuando lo bauticé de 20 años en Solentiname
porque quería pasar de su protestantismo alienado de allí
a nuestro cristianismo revolucionario
no quiso tener un padrino y una madrina
todo el Club Juvenil campesino fueron sus padrinos y madrinas.
        Sobre todo su obsesión por la Revolución.
Fascinado con el marxismo pero sin querer nunca leerlo.
Muy inteligente, pero sin querer formarse intelectualmente.
La persona más mal hablada que he conocido.
Pero el que decía las "malas palabras" con más pureza.
Una vez, comentando el Evangelio en la misa:
      "Esos Magos la cagaron llegando donde Herodes".
O, sobre la Santísima Trinidad (su resumen):
      "Los tres jodidos son uno solo."
La noche que me confesó frente a la calmura del lago:
      "Ya no creo en Dios ni en ninguna de esas mierdas.
      Creo en Dios pero para mí Dios es el hombre".
Pero siempre quiso ser mi monaguillo en la misa.
      Nadie le podía quitar ese puesto.
Su expresión más frecuente: ME VALE VERGA.
Hijo mío y hermano Laureano,
      hijo indócil y cariñoso
como todo hijo con su padre
y como además yo no era tu verdadero padre
fuiste sobre todo mi hermano

A Very Screwed Up Trip

That unexpected phone call from Managua
              to the last island of the Antilles:
    "Ernesto, Laureano died."
On the Trinidad-Barbados-Jamaica-Havana-Managua flight
        Looking at the sea, and more sea, I could think of nothing else.
Since we were born hopeless and hapless
it would be best to die a Hero and Martyr
       as you died.
Of course it would be better that you would never die,
as long as your wife and your children and your friends and the whole world
never died.
When I baptized you at the age of 20 in Solentiname
because you wanted to pass from that alienated Protestantism of yours
to our revolutionary Christianity
you didn't want to have one godfather and one godmother
the whole peasant Youth Club was your godfather and godmother.
        Above all your obsession with the Revolution.
Fascinated with Marxism but without ever wanting to read about it.
Very intelligent, but without wishing any intellectual formation.
The worst-mouthed person I have ever known.
But the one who said the "bad words" with the most purity.
Once, at Mass commenting on the Gospel:
    "Those Wise Men fucked up by going to Herod."
Or, on the Holy Trinity (your summary):
    "All three bastards are just one."
The night you confessed to me by the calm of the lake:
    "Now I don't believe in God or in any of this shit.
    I believe in God but for me God is people."
But you always wanted to be my altar boy at Mass.
    No one could take the post from you.
Your most frequent expression: I DON'T GIVE A FUCK.
My son and brother Laureano,
        intractable and affectionate
like every son with his father
and since I was also not your real father
you were above all my brother

hermano bastante menor en años
                    pero sobre todo compañero
¿esa palabra te gusta más verdad?
            La que más amabas después de la palabra Revolución.
Compañero Sub-Comandante Laureano,
            Jefe de los Guarda Fronteras:
Digo junto con vos, que nos vale verga la muerte.
            No quería hacer este poema.
Pero me dirías en aquel tu lenguaje poético de aquellas misas
traducido después a tantos idiomas, hasta el japonés
                                (les costará traducirte):
"Poeta hijueputa decí a esos jodidos mis compañeros de Solentiname
que me mataron los contrarrevolucionarios hijos de la gran puta
pero que me vale verga".
            Como aquel "que se rinda tu madre" de Leonel.
Siempre me decías allá que querías ya irte a la guerrilla.
Y yo: "Con tu indisciplina allí te fusilan".
Hasta que se te cumplió tu sueño con el asalto a San Carlos.
            "Aquí los vamos a joder a estos jodidos".
Las balas que te tiraban los guardias. Y tu relato después:
"¡Pas! ¡Pas! ¡Pas! ¡Puta! Allí fue cuando me sentí muerto".
Pendenciero, fiestero, mujerero,
rebosante de vida pero sin temer la muerte.
Poco antes de morir me había dicho tranquilo en Managua:
"Allí es encachimbado. Cualquier día yo puedo morir en una emboscada".
No has dejado de existir:
Has existido siempre
y existirás siempre
                (no sólo en este,
            en todos los universos).
Pero es cierto,
una sola vez viviste,
                    pensaste,
                        amaste.
Y ahora estás muerto.
Es estar digamos como la tierra, o la piedra, que es lo mismo,
"la piedra dura porque esa ya no siente".
Pero no, nada de piedra dura,
sí estás sintiendo,
            más allá de la velocidad de la luz
                del final del espacio que es el tiempo,
totalmente consciente,
                    dentro de la conciencia
vivicísima
            de todo lo existente.

brother much the younger in years
                but above all compañero
this word you like the most, right?
                The one you loved most after the word Revolution.
Compañero Sub-Commander Laureano,
                Chief of the Frontier Guards:
I say along with you, that we don't give a fuck about death.
                I didn't want to write this poem.
But you would tell me in that poetic language of yours in those Masses
translated later into so many languages, even Japanese
                                (they'd pay dear translating you):
"Poet, son of a bitch, tell all my fucked up compañeros from Solentiname
that the sons of the great whore counterrevolutionaries killed me
but I don't give a fuck."
                Like that "let your mother surrender" of Leonel.
You always told me there that you were ready to join the guerrillas.
And I: "With your lack of discipline, they'll execute you."
Then your dream was fulfilled with the assault on San Carlos.
                "Here we're going to fuck over these fuckers."
The shots the guards fired at you. And your version afterwards:
"Bam! Bam! Bam! Bitch! That's when I felt dead."
Troublemaker, life of the party, womanizer,
brimming with life but not fearing death.
A short time before you died you had told me calmly in Managua:
"It's fucked up out there. Any day I could die in an ambush."
You have not ceased to exist:
You have always existed
and you shall exist forever
                (not only in this universe,
                        but in all of them).
But it's certain,
that only once did you live
                        did you think,
                        did you love.
And now you are dead.
It's being, let's say, like the earth, or a rock, which is the same thing,
"the hard rock because it no longer feels."
But no, nothing of hard rock,
you *do* feel,
        beyond the velocity of light
                beyond the end of space that is time,
totally conscious,
                within consciousness
fully alive
        to all that exists.

LAUREANO MAIRENA ¡PRESENTE!

El jodido avión retrasándose en cada escala.
Ya era muy noche en el mar. Yo no podía dejar de pensar . . .
Yo quisiera morir como vos hermano Laureano
y mandar a decir desde lo que llamamos cielo
"Rejodidos hermanos míos de Solentiname, me valió verga la muerte".

LAUREANO MAIRENA! PRESENT!

The fucked up plane getting later with each landing.
Now it was late night in the sea. I couldn't help thinking . . .
I would like to die like you brother Laureano
and send word from the place we call heaven,
"My fucked over brothers from Solentiname, I didn't give a fuck about
death."

Ante una foto

Combatiente del Frente Sandinista
que estás en esta foto con tu pistola
                    apuntando al enemigo
con el pañuelo roji-negro en el rostro
cubriéndote hasta un poco más abajo de los ojos
          parapetado detrás de un muro
con la mirada fija y el arma firmemente apretada
en dirección al enemigo:
Muchas cosas pasaron en ese combate,
                    no sabemos cuál combate,
muchas más siguieron pasando. Ya ganamos.
          Ya fue el 19 de Julio.
Muchas cosas grandes ha habido desde entonces,
y seguirán habiendo cosas grandes.
          Vendrán nuevas generaciones.
Pero vos estarás siempre así, de 18 años,
detrás de un murito, valiente, tenso, immóvil
          eterno
apuntando al enemigo.

Before a Photo

Combatant of the Sandinista Front
in this photo with your pistol
                aiming at the enemy
with the red and black kerchief over your face
covering yourself up to just a bit below the eyes
        protected behind a wall
with your fixed stare and your weapon firmly grasped
pointing toward the enemy:
Many things happened in this battle,
                we don't know which battle,
many more continued taking place. Now we have won.
        Now the 19th of July has taken place.
Many great things have happened since then,
and great things will continue to happen.
        New generations will come.
But you will always be as you are, 18 years old,
behind a small wall, courageous, tense, still
        eternal
aiming at the enemy.

En la tumba del guerrillero

Pienso en tu cuerpo que se ha ido desbaratando bajo la tierra
haciéndose suave tierra, humus otra vez
junto con el humus de todos los demás humanos
que han existido y existirán en la bolita del mundo
haciéndonos todos juntos tierra fértil del planeta Tierra.
Y cuando los cosmonautas miren esta bola azul y rosa
                              en la noche negra
lo que estarán mirando, lejos, es tu luminosa tumba
      (tu tumba y la de todos)
y cuando los extraterrestres desde alguna parte
         miren este punto de luz de la Tierra
estarán mirando tu tumba.
Y un día será todo tumba, silenciosa tumba,
y ya no habrá más seres vivos en el planeta compañero.
    ¿Y después?
Después nos desbarataremos más, volaremos, átomos en el cosmos.
Y tal vez la materia es eterna hermano
sin principio ni fin o tiene un fin y recomienza cada vez.
Tu amor sí tuvo un comienzo pero no tiene final.
Y tus átomos que estuvieron en el suelo de Nicaragua,
tus átomos amorosos, que dieron la vida por amor,
ya verás, serán luz,
me imagino tus partículas en la vastedad del cosmos como pancartas
como afiches vivos.
        No sé si me explico.
Lo que sé es que nunca se olvidará tu nombre
y para siempre se gritará: ¡Presente!

In the Tomb of the Guerrilla Fighter

I think of your body that has been falling apart beneath the earth
becoming soft dirt, humus once more
together with the humus of all the other humans
who have existed or will exist on this small ball of the world
all of us together becoming the fertile earth of this planet Earth.
And when the cosmonauts see this blue and pink ball
          in the black night
what they'll be seeing, far away, is your luminous tomb
  (your tomb and the tomb of everyone)
and when extraterrestials from some place
    see this point of light from the Earth
they'll be seeing your tomb.
And one day it will be all tomb, silent tomb,
and then there will no longer be any living being on this planet, compañero.
  And afterwards?
Afterwards we'll fall apart more, we'll fly, atoms in the cosmos.
And perhaps matter is eternal, brother,
without beginning or end or it has an end and starts again each time.
Your love surely had a beginning but has no end.
And your atoms that were in the soil of Nicaragua,
your loving atoms, that gave their life for love,
you'll see, they'll be light,
I imagine your particles in the vastness of the cosmos like signs
like living posters.
     I don't know if I explain myself.
What I know is that your name will never be forgotten
and that "Present!" will be shouted forever.

19 de Julio

En el planeta vuelve a ser otra vez 19 de Julio,
            otra vez después del triunfo,
esto es:
el 19 de Julio va dando vueltas por todo el planeta
y va dando vueltas por todo el planeta el amanecer,
mejor dicho, el planeta va dando vueltas ante el amanecer,
            este amanecer del 19 de Julio,
y el pedazo nuestro Nicaragua pasa hacia el mediodía
con la Plaza 19 de Julio repleta de pueblo bajo el sol
todos los colores en ella como repleta de flores
y va pasando más, hacia el cono de la sombra,
            el cono de la noche con estrellas,
y ya brillan las primeras estrellas
            sobre la Plaza 19 de Julio,
ellas con otras fechas de otros calendarios de otras órbitas.
¿Habrá allá un planeta bajo una lluvia contínua?
            ¿O tendrá ya dinosaurios?
            ¿O ya es el Reino de los Cielos?
¿Y cómo se nos verá desde allá?
            ¡Como una de esas estrellas!
Qué bella se verá entre ellas nuestra Tierra.

19th of July

On our planet it has come around to be July 19 once more,
           once more after the victory,
that is:
the 19th of July goes turning around the whole planet
and spinning around the whole planet goes the dawn,
or let's say, the planet goes spinning before the dawn,
           this dawn of July 19,
and this little bit of ours our Nicaragua passes by around noon
with the July 19 Plaza filled with people under the sun
all the colors in it as if filled with flowers
and it goes passing by more, towards the cone of shadows,
           the cone of night with stars,
and the first stars already shine
                      over the July 19 Plaza,
those with other dates from other calendars from other orbits.
Could there be a planet out there under a continuous rain?
           Or could it already have dinosaurs?
           Or has the Kingdom of Heaven already come there?
And how will they see us from there?
           Like one of these stars!
How beautiful our Earth will look among them.

Visión de la ventanilla azul

En la ventanita redonda, todo es azul,
tierra azulosa, verde-azul, azul
      (y cielo)
   todo es azul
lago y lagunas azules
     volcanes azules
mientras más lejos la tierra más azul
   islas azules en lago azul.
Éste es el rostro de la tierra liberada.
Y donde todo el pueblo peleó, pienso:
      ¡para el amor!
Vivir sin el odio
    de la explotación.
Para amarnos en una tierra bella
muy bella, no sólo por ella
    sino por los hombres en ella,
sobre todo por los hombres en ella.
Por eso nos la dió Dios bella
para la sociedad en ella.
Y en todos esos sitios azules se peleó, se sufrió
   para una sociedad de amor
     aquí en esta tierra.
Un trozo azul tiene mayor intensidad . . .
Y me pareció estar viendo allí los lugares de todos los combates,
y de todas las muertes,
detrás de ese vidrio redondo, pequeño,
      azul
   todos los tonos de azul.

Vision from the Blue Window

From the round window, everything is blue,
the earth bluish, blue-green, blue
                              (sky-blue)
            everything is blue
blue lakes and lagoons
                  blue volcanoes
the further away the land, the bluer it is
      blue islands in a blue lake.
This is the face of the liberated land.
And where all the people fought, I think:
                              for love!
To live without exploitation's
                        hatred.
To love each other in a lovely land
very lovely, not only for the land
            but for its people
above all for its people.
That's why God rendered it so lovely
for its society.
And in all those blue places they fought, they suffered
          for a society of love
                        here in this land.
A bit of blue has greater intensity . . .
And it seemed to me I was seeing the places of all the battles,
and all the deaths,
that, behind this glass, small, round,
                              blue
            I was seeing all the shades of blue.